SPRING

BOUNCING BACK FROM

REJECTION

SPRING

BOUNCING BACK FROM

REJECTION

Ambi Parameswaran

First published by Westland Business, an imprint of Westland Publications Private Limited, in 2020

Published by Westland Business, an imprint of Westland Books, a division of Nasadiya Technologies Private Limited, in 2022

No. 269/2B, First Floor, 'Irai Arul', Vimalraj Street, Nethaji Nagar, Allappakkam Main Road, Maduravoyal, Chennai 600095

Westland, the Westland logo, Westland Business and the Westland Business logo are the trademarks of Nasadiya Technologies Private Limited, or its affiliates.

ISBN: …

10 9 8 7 6 5 4 3 2 1

Typeset by SÜRYA, New Delhi

Printed at …

*This book is dedicated to the many rejections I faced in my career.
Each of a different colour, and each teaching me
some valuable new lessons.*

*This book is also dedicated to the brave student
who asked me to confess my rejection stories.*

CONTENTS

The Oxford Dictionary defines a 'spring' as 'a twisted piece of metal that can be pushed, pressed or pulled but which always returns to its original shape or position afterwards'.

A metal wire can be made into a 'spring' so that it can bounce back to its original form however much it is pushed, pressed or pulled.

This book is about trying to find out the 'spring' in each and every one of us. How can we face rejection and failure in our work lives and yet bounce back to our original shape?

To go a step further can we use each rejection to become a little bit better? May be a 'super spring' that gets better the more it is pushed, pressed or pulled!

Read on to find out more about how you can become a Super Spring!

INTRODUCTION

Facing, Processing and Learning from Rejection

Strength does not come from physical capacity.
It comes from an indomitable will.

—Mahatma Gandhi

Why a book called *Spring* on the topic of 'rejection', you may well ask? Let me start with what triggered my quest towards understanding rejection. I have faced a fair share of rejection in my work life and have also helped my coachees manage rejection as they navigate their developmental journey. I have also read what experts and psychologists have to say about how we anticipate, face and handle rejection. But the book's idea did not come from any epiphany while reading a learned article. It was triggered by an innocent question posed to me by a young girl.

Here is the complete backstory.

In October 2018, I was invited by Jagran Lake University in Bhopal to talk to their mass communication students about my experience in the world of marketing and advertising. My talk centered on my previous book *Sponge—Leadership Lessons I Learnt From My Clients*. The talk was well appreciated by the 200+ students and their professors who had assembled in the auditorium. As is the normal practice, after the talk there was an extra thirty minutes allotted for a question-and-answer session. A number of questions were asked by the attendees that covered various aspects of client relationships, the complexities of the advertising business, how the world of marketing is changing and so on. As we kept giving an opportunity for more and more students to ask questions, from the back of the hall one hand kept staying up. We finally went to this persistent girl who had been feverishly wanting to ask a question. And feverish she was.

Her question was, 'Sir, you have had a great career. You had a great education and you went on to work in some excellent companies with some truly visionary leaders. And you were very successful in what you set out to do. But sir, we are youngsters here. We are entering the world of business, marketing and media with a lot of fear. We are worried that we will have to face rejection in what we are attempting to do.' In short, what she was asking me was:

What can you tell us that can help us handle rejection?
Or how did you handle rejection?

The question was not something that I was expecting to hear, after what I hoped had been an inspirational talk about how we could all become leaders if we continuously learnt from our customers and clients. This question, however, was a lot more basic and fundamental. And in a sense it touched a raw nerve. I could sense that the mood of the audience resonated with her question as she explained her point in great detail.

I could literally hear the audience saying to themselves, this guy had it all. He was lucky to get into some good institutes, and managed to get a good job. He makes it all sound so easy. Get a good degree, get a great job, and then keep learning. But real life is not so easy. He seems to be glossing over the complexities of achieving success. Maybe, he is a bit of a fraud. A trickster who is painting an overly rosy picture and not sharing the real challenges of succeeding in the world of business.

I took a deep breath. And started speaking about 'rejection'; about how just because I was fortunate enough to have had some good educational qualifications, I had to face lesser rejections initially. But that being said, once I entered the work force, I faced plenty of rejection and failure. From my first job to the first campaign I managed and much else besides, rejection had been a part and parcel of my life. I shared some of those moments. And I don't know what happened, as I finished my mini-talk on 'managing rejection', the entire audience stood up to give me a standing ovation.

Mind you, I did not get a standing ovation when I finished my sixty-minute talk on 'leadership lessons' but I got one after my ten-minute discourse on rejection.

This got me thinking. What had really happened there? Why were the students so worried about rejection? And what did I say that managed to connect with them and hit the right note?

Everyone has rejection and failure fears

Worries about rejection and failure are not just confined to the youngsters, such as the girl who asked me the question, but also those who are significantly older. Some may be running their own businesses or trying to start out on their own. Or they may be in mid-level jobs in good or not-so-good organisations. While the younger lot are worried about getting the right job, the slightly older lot are worried about growth, promotion and job enrichment. While the two generations may be separated by a decade or more, there are many similarities between these two generations in terms of anxieties and ambitions.

The millennials, as demographers tell us, are those born in the mid-1980s who are now making progress in their career journey. The next generation, born in the early 2000s (often called Gen-i) are in college and trying to figure out the future as this book is being written in the year 2020. There are some similarities between these two generations. Both these generations, at least the middle/upper-middle class boys and girls from urban centres of India, have seen India grow rapidly. They have seen their homes getting filled steadily with newer and newer gadgets. Many or most of them are probably from nuclear families, with one sibling, at best. Their parents have devoted a huge amount of time and resources to get them the best education possible. So in a sense they have lived a cocooned existence. That is their story till they enter undergraduate education in a college. Their life changes when they move out of a familiar school to an unfamiliar college. Add to this the likelihood that they are apprehensive that everything will change when they leave college. They, perhaps, feel ill-prepared to face the challenges. And the word 'rejection' sends shivers down their spine.

What is rejection anyway?

Let us try and understand what I mean by the term 'rejection' and its many different shades.

During their last years of undergraduate or graduate education, the rejection worries faced by students could be one or many of these:

- Will I get selected to the team that will represent the institute in a competition?
- Will I get relegated to a second-level team and hence suffer rejection?
- Will I get shortlisted by the company (of my dreams) for an interview?
- Will I get rejected at the interview stage?
- Will I get the right job assignment or will I get a not-so-good job assignment?
- What happens if my first job is a dead-end one?

Well, rejection is not just something that only youngsters are worried about. Rejection looms large in the work environment too. After you start working, you are worried if you will get a better assignment. Or that your dream proposal will get rejected.

As you start your career you have multiple 'rejection fears' and some of them are as below:

- Will my proposal get rejected by the senior management?

- Will my sales pitch get rejected by the client?
- Will my boss reject my ideas?
- Will my colleagues reject my suggestions?
- Will I get selected for better postings inside the company?
- Will I be keeping pace with my fellow batchmates?
- Will I get promoted next year?

If you are thinking of starting your own venture, you are worried that your proposal will get rejected by angel investors, and later by venture capital firms. How many rejections will you have to face before you make it big? Will the talent you want to hire reject your offer? And so on.

Getting rejected is something that worries everyone. And somehow it seems to be a big black hole that can swallow you, in full.

But the truth is that the most successful of people you know have had to go through rejection multiple times in their lives. Someone whom you think was a born leader probably got rejected many times before he landed the right job. Numerous bestselling authors have had to submit their manuscripts to multiple publishers before someone decided to risk their reputation by publishing a first-time author. The same is true of some of the biggest movies and television programmes. Movie stars who have won multiple Oscar awards, who have numerous hits under their belt, have all faced rejection. The top musicians and those whom we see today as demigods of music have all faced rejection. Some of the top athletes have been dropped from teams when they were in good form. Senior government servants have had to face rejection right through their career. Entrepreneurs have their own share of rejection stories to share.

Kris Gopalakrishnan is one of the founders of the IT services giant, Infosys. I had visited him some years ago in connection with an event at IIT Madras. I was greatly impressed as I walked into the Infosys campus in Bangalore's Electronic City. Infosys was started by a team of engineers who all hailed from typical Indian middle-class families. So if they could create such a great company, what is stopping all of us, I wondered. I mentioned this to Kris when we got talking and congratulated him and Team Infosys for creating a company that is today a shining example of Indian information technology entrepreneurship. Kris was quick to point out that for the first ten years of their existence Infosys had to face numerous rejections. While Infosys is a stock market darling today and has been for well over two decades, its initial public offering (IPO) was met with a lukewarm response and had to get its underwriters/bankers to pick up the unsubscribed portion of the issue. But if someone had invested Rs 10,000 in 1993 at the time of the Infosys IPO, they would have been richer by more than Rs 2 crores on the twenty-fifth anniversary of the IPO. That translates into a two-thousand multiple in twenty-five years, outclassing any other form of investment.

So some of the biggest successes we see around us have had to battle multiple rejections.

My struggles with rejection

What qualifies me to write on the subject of rejection could be a question that may be going through your mind just about now.

In 2019, I completed forty years of working in coaching, consulting, marketing, advertising and general management. Of the forty years, I spent thirty-five years in corporate India across four organisations and had to face a fair share of rejection. And in the last five years, I have been engaged as an Executive Coach with high-performance managers many of whom are struggling to cope with rejection. In that sense, I have had a ringside view of rejection, from both sides, over the last forty years.

So to rest your fears, let me enumerate a few rejections that I had to face in my forty-year career in marketing, advertising, sales and consulting/coaching:

- I was rejected by one of the biggest FMCG firms when I applied to them for a job from campus; *not once but twice.*
- I did not get the promotion that I thought I richly deserved; *more than once.*
- The draft of my first book of advertising cases was thought to be more an agency promotion puff-piece by an eminent professor of integrated marketing communication, who in fact was sure that no publisher would be interested in it.
- Several clients have rejected campaign ideas that I have presented to them, *multiple times.*
- In fact, one client 'sacked' me and our ad agency, for what I thought was no fault of ours.
- Several important new business ideas were rejected by prospective clients

And I can go on.

As you can see I have faced my fair share of rejections. Some of them set me back quite a bit. Some got me to readjust my priorities. Some of them made me all the more determined to chase the end goal.

But the big learning for me, as I reflect back on my journey in the world of business is that there is no one magic bullet to handle rejection. I have seen successful colleagues handle rejection very differently from the way I would have. I have had some insightful moments after facing a crippling rejection. An epiphany or two.

The common advice seems to be that don't let rejection set you back. Keep trying and you will succeed, eventually. This piece of advice seems to be rather tame. It's a bland thing to tell a young person who is worried about his or her career and job.

Are there multiple ways to handle rejection? Are there situations where you have to be prepared to be rejected and have a Plan B in your pocket? Can you see rejection as a positive step for you to move ahead? Can a rejection open new doors for you to explore?

My research on the topic of rejection unearthed many interesting facts and factoids. Almost every book on self-development has a chapter devoted to 'handling rejection'. So I thought why not devote an entire book on rejection?

Becoming a SPRING that can bounce back after being pushed or pulled

In the chapters that follow, I have tried to delve into my own stories of rejection and what I did to handle the rejection I faced. I have also taken the liberty of referring to stories I have heard from colleagues and friends on how they handled rejection. In the process of writing and researching this book, I met with and spoke to Olympic athletes, senior retired IAS officers, respected academics, veteran CEO coaches, musicians and artists. You will meet famous people, scientists and authors who had their own recipes for handling rejection.

In addition, I also delved into numerous books and articles on the subject of rejection, resilience and failure.

I found that while rejection is just one word, every rejection is different. No two rejections are the same. As Leo Tolstoy said in *Anna Karenina,* 'Happy families are all alike; every unhappy family is unhappy in its own way.'

Just as every rejection is different, the way you handle the rejection needs to be different too. And the way you will handle the rejection may be different from the way your friend would handle it.

The book will give you a template to analyse rejection. And hopefully the book will give you a few new ways of handling rejection. You may have to develop your own variant of a method that I have enumerated here. You may then identify a new way in which you could have handled a rejection in the past.

The book will also make you sit up and look at rejection with new eyes. Can you look at a rejection as a positive outcome? Is it possible that the rejection made you refocus to get to a better place?

Irrespective of the stage of life you are at, a student, a young executive, an executive facing a midlife crisis, a businessman facing challenges, or a start-up hotshot worried about the next meeting with the VC, rejection is something you will face. Again and again.

Can you allow rejection to defeat you? Or can you make rejection work in your favour?

When you are rejected, what is really rejected? Your idea? Or you as a person? Can you distance yourself from the idea, and so not take rejection personally?

Not getting that dream job is a downer. Sure. But is it the end of the road?

Not getting the promotion is a big disappointment. But should that make you look for a new job?

Being rejected by VC Number 10 is a killer. Will you continue to plough ahead or will you go back to the drawing board?

Getting ready to build your internal SPRING: Anticipating and facing; processing and recovering; learning and progressing

While there is no magic potion to handle rejection, I have organised the book in three parts: Anticipating and Facing Rejection; Processing and Recovering from Rejection; and Learning and Progressing after Rejection. The chapters have been arranged broadly in line with the key motif or the key story that is being presented in the chapter. While each chapter does present a complete story of how a rejection was faced and how it was handled, as you progress through the book you will find that the tenor changes ever so slightly to take you deeper into the topic.

Just as a spring manufacturing process had three stages: coiling the wire into a spring; hardening the spring; and finally polishing the spring, you too will traverse through stories and concepts that help you understand the importance of anticipating rejection, processing rejection and learning from rejection.

The eighteen chapters that are grouped into three parts, while having a broad sequence, can be read in any order.

As I said in Bhopal on that day, you cannot let rejection take the wind out of your sails. Yes, you have to be prepared to face rejection. Life is not a bed of roses. There are multiple thorns for you to handle. But remember, a rejection may be a positive sign.

The book largely deals with work life but the stories and lessons in the book are equally applicable to your personal life too. A rejection may be a blessing. And another rejection may just be a 'buying signal', a signal that the prospect is ready to buy, but is not saying 'yes' as yet.

In the movie *Gone with the Wind*, the lead character Scarlett O'Hara has this to say at the end of the book, after her beau Rhett Butler leaves her: 'I will think of another way of getting him back. After all, tomorrow is another day.'

You have an internal SPRING. This SPRING helps you take setbacks and gets you back on your feet. This book will help you discover your SPRING, to make it a little more agile and 'springy'. So that you can spring back with a smile on your face when you are hit by a rejection.

part one

ANTICIPATING AND FACING REJECTION

A helical compression spring is an open-pitch spring which is used to resist applied compression forces or to store energy.

—Standard Handbook of Machine Design

Coiling is the first step in the creation of a spring. Wire is either coiled at room temperature around a shaft called an arbor or mandrel; or is coiled without a mandrel using a CNC machine.

Blowing a Job Interview and Finding a New Path

Every time I thought I was being rejected from something good,
I was actually being redirected to something better.

—Steve Maraboli, author and motivational speaker

The year 1977 was interesting in many ways. It was the year that the country was put back on the democratic path once again, after two years of emergency rule. It was also the year that I graduated from IIT Madras. It will be difficult for the young readers to believe that placement time even at the IITs during the 1970s wasn't exactly brimming with recruiters. I was not a top-ranking student and therefore did not aspire to head to the US for graduate studies, as many of my fellow chemical engineers were doing. So I cycled up to the Placement Office to find out if there were any good companies visiting the campus.

To my pleasant surprise, Hindustan Lever (or HLL as it was known then, now Hindustan Unilever) was visiting the campus and, lo and behold, had asked for chemical engineering students. I put together my CV and trooped back to the Placement Office for my interview a few days later. I should admit, I was firmly in the middle of the class of forty and thought I would be able to answer the questions the recruiters may have for me (most of the top rankers were going to the US anyway).

There were around twenty of us applying. But I got out on the first ball. I fumbled with the first two questions so badly that I was shooed out very quickly. The question that I struggled to answer was a simple one as I was to discover later. It was to create a simple device to ensure that a liquid drum would not overflow. I got confused and kept rambling on. Later in the day, I discovered that the answer was the first diagram in the textbook we had used in the 'Chemical Engineering Unit Operations' course. All you needed was an outlet pipe at the level below overflow. Something I suspect a school student may have answered.

Clearly, all the chemical engineering thermodynamics I had studied had addled my brain. I also learnt that day that many of the recruiters who come from big companies have only a limited storehouse of questions (the HR guys especially). So HLL was off the table.

The next interview with Sriram Fibres went better and I managed to land an Engineering Trainee job for a glorious monthly stipend of Rs 800.

With that back-up plan in place, I chased my dream of doing an MBA at a good institute. When I got an acceptance call from IIM Calcutta, I accepted it immediately and also told the Placement Office of IIT Madras that they should thank Sriram Fibres and inform them that I was heading to Calcutta (now Kolkata).

Exactly one year after the first rejection from HLL, I was set to meet them once again. This time it was for a summer internship as a first year MBA student from IIM. HLL was the hottest marketing company and so there was a big queue of applicants for the summer internship offer. More than forty of my fellow IIMCites had applied (of a total of around hundred). The final round was reduced to just the two of us. I was happy that I had made it to the final two, but was a little cocky since I was also a top ranking student at IIMC (some of my IITM friends till date don't believe that I could have risen so high so fast academically, but that is the topic for another book). HLL did not want two summer interns and so there was a shoot-out of sorts between the two shortlisted candidates.

That day I learnt yet another lesson about HR teams that companies send to campuses. But back to the shoot-out.

I walked in to the room for what I was told was the final question. I sat down and looked at the interviewers with eager eyes and ears. One of them took off his wristwatch and gave it to me and said 'Sell this back to me!'. I looked at the watch, then at the interviewer, then again at the watch. I then began to hold forth about the utility value of a wristwatch, its style etc. They asked me to stop at some stage and I walked out thinking that I had done a great job.

My friend who walked in after me was asked the same question. To which he answered, 'Thank you, gentlemen, for the watch. If you want it back you have to pay me for it.' Needless to say, he landed the assignment.

We were friends and so he told me what he had done, and honestly I thought he deserved the internship for his chutzpah.

I had been rejected by the most treasured recruiter at IIMC. I did not sleep that night. My friends, who were all rooting for me, did their best to console me. I was kicking myself for not thinking of a clever way of answering the question. But the truth was that it was a coin toss with a twist. I could have felt happy that I had made it to the last two and concluded that the better of the two won. That was not the case. At least on the day that it had happened.

What would you have done if you had faced such a rejection? Would you have resolved that you would never apply to HLL again? Would you have resolved that the next time you faced HLL you would be even more prepared? But honestly, how prepared can you be if the questions that come your way are 'bouncers'?

I did some more soul searching after that rejection. What was I looking for from my education? What would be of value as I finished my two years at IIM Calcutta?

What are you chasing?

For a minute, I would like to digress from my story to point out the problem of creating a 'dream company' early on in your studies. I notice that in several business schools students are encouraged to identify a dream company that they want to work in, as early as in the first semester. They are then told to focus all their projects around that company. Hopefully, they will be able to land a job with their dream company. But what if they don't? What if they get a 'bouncer' in the last round of interviews?

I feel creating a dream company early in the education journey, in business schools, or law schools or engineering schools or whichever school you may be studying in is the wrong way to go. Education should be broad and while you may have one or two or three so-called dream companies, you should never get so obsessed that you ignore all other options that may be on offer. And as this section of the book asserts, you have to anticipate rejection. Never be sure of getting through.

Back to my soul searching in early 1978. It soon dawned on me that I did not know Calcutta and I should use the summer to explore Calcutta. I should use the rejection to try and move in a new direction.

From lusting after a summer assignment in a top FMCG company, I redirected my efforts towards landing a summer assignment that would let me stay on in Calcutta and get to understand the city a little better. I remember Pond's India (Madras-based then) came looking, but I did not apply. Neither did I apply for Godrej & Boyce.

Those days summer internship interviews were not bunched into a few days. Companies tended to land up at random intervals right through the months of February and March. So almost near the end of March I noticed that an ad agency was looking for summer interns who were willing to work out of Calcutta. I had not heard of the ad agency, but thought I ought to apply.

That was the first time I met with Ajit Balakrishnan and Subhas Chakravarthy. Both were IIMC graduates and were directors of a new ad agency called Rediffusion Advertising. Ajit was the co-founder director and Subhas was the Calcutta Branch Director. I don't think there was any one else applying for that internship (a small and unknown company, a relatively less-known industry). Maybe I was foolhardy. Maybe I was just too confident. Thinking back, I applied knowing very little.

But in the interview, I got mighty impressed with what Ajit and Subhas had to say about the role of an MBA in advertising. And the whole business of advertising seemed greatly cerebral and at the same time multifarious.

I ended up doing my summer internship in 1978 at Rediffusion Calcutta. I was given the freedom to come to office when I deemed fit, but I had to give a weekly update on what I had learnt. The topic of my summer project was 'Building a Simulation Model for Media Planning'. I read up numerous articles on the topic, spending endless hours in the IIM library and I managed to unearth some interesting media planning models (that I ended up using in my real job a year later).

During the two month internship, I got to see the Calcutta office of Rediffusion from up close. Those days Rediffusion operated with a centralised creative team which was based out of Bombay (now Mumbai). The branch managers went to Bombay to get their creatives done. It was then their job to 'sell' it to their clients. I saw some terrific campaigns hot off the press—Jenson & Nicholson's 'Whenever You See Colour Think Of Us'; Red Eveready's 'The Chosen One For Your Transistor'; *New Delhi*—the Indian version of *Esquire* magazine that had a provocative set of ads with headlines such as 'Indira Gandhi's Contribution to India's Night Life—The Mid-Night Knock' (on the Emergency).

During those two months, I also spent time roaming around Calcutta exploring its music and book shops. Jayanta Sengupta of Rediffusion took me to my first jazz concert. Alok Kumar showed me a rolled-up canvas of a Jamini Roy painting he had sourced for Rediffusion managing director,

Arun Nanda. I discovered Mama's Kitchen and its authentic Chinese dhaba food. Nizam's rolls. And I can go on. Two months went by in a jiffy. My project report was done and handed over to Subhas Chakravarty who gave me a pat on my head saying, 'Well done, my boy.'

I had made a lot of new friends and so the following ten months I made it a habit to visit Rediffusion Calcutta regularly. I even helped carry some furniture when they were shifting offices.

Cut to March 1979. I got a call from Subhas on a Saturday asking if I was free that evening for a chat and a drink. I landed up at our favourite watering hole at New Kenilworth Hotel. The next two, or was it three, hours were spent discussing how the world of advertising was changing. And how Rediffusion was blazing a new trail in the world of Indian advertising. The entry of MBAs into advertising had started a few years earlier, but it was the rise of Rediffusion that gave this phenomenon fresh momentum.

Clients were happy to see their own types (MBAs) on the other side of the table. The agency world till then was dominated by the English theatrewalas. So it was a dramatic shift. Rediffusion had picked up some great new accounts and had also attracted some terrific new leaders. P.S. 'Vish' Viswanathan in Bombay. R. 'Naru' Narayanan in Madras (now Chennai). Sheila Sircar in Delhi. And many others.

Finally, Subhas asked me if I would be interested in joining Rediffusion in May 1979 as a Management Trainee. I think I was expecting the offer at some stage of the conversation. So I asked him, 'Is this an offer?' He replied that he had been empowered by the MD and Ajit to make the offer. I realised that after my 'stellar' record at interviews, I was finally landing this job without any real interview. I quickly said 'yes'. Subhas offered to give me time to think it over. But I think I was somehow warming up for this over the previous twelve months. The answer was a quick 'yes'.

The next day when I discussed the Rediffusion offer with my close friends they were very concerned. I was a tad overqualified for the job in their opinion. What was an IIT engineer going to do in an ad agency, they wondered. I had to tell them that most marketing jobs (selling soaps or selling paint) didn't really need engineering. Why is a 'topper' like you, who can get into HLL or Nestle or Citibank aiming so low, they asked. But somehow I felt that I was making the right choice. You may call it youthful exuberance. Or naivety. But the deed was done.

Meanwhile, the placement secretary Vasant Nangia reminded me that HLL was visiting the campus the following day and they had shortlisted me (once again!). It would be improper for me not to appear for the interview, it was implied. The only way out was that Rediffusion should send their offer letter to the Placement Office before twelve noon the following day.

This led to a series of hurried phone calls on the Calcutta landline network which was patchy at best in those days. But, finally, the letter arrived (I discovered that I was going to be getting a stipend of Rs 1400 per month only after I got my copy of the letter), and I was told by the Placement Secretary to recuse myself from the HLL interview.

Perhaps, I would have been lucky the third time with HLL. But that was not to be.

I joined advertising in May 1979, thanks to the 'Rejection to Redirection' move I made in March 1978. I got to work with some terrific people in Rediffusion, some of whom you have met earlier in this chapter, the others whom you may have met in one of my other books including Arun Kale, Kamlesh Pandey, Ramesh Mulye, Ashok Kurien, Rajiv Agarwal, N. Raghunath, H.V. Prasad Subramanian, Ratha Rajiah (also an IIMC grad) and more. The three years I spend at Rediffusion was indeed a great learning experience. I then realised that I needed to do a stint in marketing; I got an offer from Boots Company (at the interview, Anil Kapoor, the Marketing Director of Boots spoke for both of us and so my terrific interviewing skills were not tested). I got back to advertising in 1989, and stayed for the next twenty-seven years. Having a lot of fun along the way.

Did my tryst with HLL end in 1979? Not really.

When I was in FCB Ulka, I was given the task of managing Wipro's Santoor. I started working on the brand in 1994 and was closely associated with the brand right through 1994 to 2016. In those twenty-plus years, we helped Santoor grow into a large powerful brand. I was especially pleased to read that Santoor had become the second largest soap brand in India in 2018, overtaking HLL or HUL's Lux. I like to please myself and wonder if this would have happened if HLL had taken me as a Summer Trainee in March 1978.

Let me stop here and ask you what you think were the lessons you learnt from that story.

I was rejected twice by a company. I had walked in without anticipating rejection. I could have tried one more time, prepared more thoroughly and possibly, I would have got the job. That was one possible way of handling the rejection. Try and try again with more gusto. And it is a perfectly acceptable way of handling rejection.

Instead of recommitting myself to landing a job in company A, or HLL in this case, I used the rejection to relook at my options. I used it to 'redirect' and put my energies in a new direction.

The power of redirection is indeed great

Let us look at a few other stories.

Arianna Huffington did not start out as the founder of *Huffington Post* (*Huff Post*). While running for the post of the Governor of California against Arnold Schwarznegger in 2003, a task she took on because she did not want the state to be hijacked by the Republicans, she came a cropper with just 2 per cent of the voters polled. It was a rejection, but she learnt a valuable lesson about herself, her communication skills and the power of the internet. She used those lessons to launch *Huff Post* and got named as one of the most influential women in media in 2009. Two years later, she sold the company to AOL for $315 million. A rejection paved the way to self-discovery and ultimately, success.

Sometimes rejection and failure never seem to go away. Mary Kay Ash sold books door to door while her husband was serving in the army. When her husband got back, they split up. Ash was left with three children to look after. Ash took up a job but got passed over for a well-deserved promotion, because she was a woman. So she and her second husband planned a business, Mary Kay Cosmetics. But her husband passed away a month before they launched. With a $5000 investment from her oldest son, Ash set sail on her new adventure. In 2014, her company Mary Kay Cosmetics was reported to have hit a turnover of $3.5 billion by *Forbes* magazine.

Sabyasachi Mukherjee is today one of the most admired fashion designers. He has become a brand in himself and L'Oreal, world's number one cosmetics company, has launched its own Sabyasachi range of colour cosmetics. But did Sabyasachi start out being a designer? In his own words he was struggling to find his voice: 'I think a lot of creative people suffer from a lack of self-expression. I was a creative person in the wrong education stream. I was studying medicine, then economics, wasn't very sure what I would do.' Dissonance drove Sabyasachi to a dark place but dressing in radical clothes helped him find his way again: 'Self-expression helped me cope with the frustrations of not being able to find a creative outlet.' He started expressing himself by dyeing his hair orange and wearing ripped jeans with safety pins in them. And slowly he discovered what he wanted to do with his life.

Imagine you make a powerful presentation to your bosses about a new idea you are passionate about. And it gets rejected.

Will you sit and lament the loss or will you use the rejection to push you in a new direction?

Let us assume that the idea you had was a perfectly good one, but your bosses did not think it was the right time to go ahead with the idea. Will you continue relentless, or will you drop the idea and move on? To a new area of exploration.

In the world of start-ups, there is a term for redirecting your effort: 'pivot'. You start with an idea which you think is a sure-fire success. But down the road you realise that it is not something that is going to work. So you don't try to fix your offer. You 'pivot'. You change direction.

Let me give you an example.

Myntra is possibly one of, if not *the* top fashion e-commerce websites in India. Today, they are part of Flipkart and hence part of Walmart. I remember IDG, their venture capital investors, inviting me to meet them during their early days, in 2007-8. They were then trying to become India's favourite e-commerce site for personalised items. Caps, t-shirts, coffee mugs and so on. They were keen on exploring corporate tie-ups and examine the potential for branded merchandise for brands. They had lined up a robust supply chain to make t-shirts, shirts, caps, bags, key-chains and were looking to become suppliers to companies. I remember connecting them with some of my clients including Tata Motors. But after struggling with this business model for almost four years, the founders of Myntra did a 180-degree pivot. They switched their business from supplying personalised items and gifts to becoming a fashion portal. Once they set their mind to it, they could build a formidable business around fashion. They got acquired by Flipkart in 2014 and then later in 2018, by Walmart when it acquired Flipkart. A news report in May 2019 says that Walmart will continue to support Myntra as a fashion portal.

That was just one example of a pivot. Some start-ups go through multiple pivots till they hit 'escape velocity'.

What is applicable to Mytra is also applicable to you, irrespective of what you are involved with.

When you are faced with rejection, what will you do?

The first step is to anticipate rejection even before you are hit by it. No, you should not be diffident and act as if you stand no chance of making it through. But in the back of your head, you should be ready to accept rejection. Don't confuse the rejection with your persona. You are not your idea. You are not your CV. So first, distance yourself from the idea. Now that you have pulled yourself out of it, start looking at it dispassionately. How committed are you to the idea? Is it really such a good idea?

We often confuse our persona with the idea we present. These are two very different concepts. Let me illustrate this by quoting a famous author.

Jayakanthan (1943-2015) is a Sahitya Akademi Award-winning Tamil author. I am a big fan of Jayakanthan and have read many of his books and enjoyed the film renditions of some of his classic novels. In the introduction to one of his novels, he speaks of common questions that his readers ask him. 'Sir, why did you not let Shobha marry Shankar? Did he not wait for her for ten years? How could you be so cruel?' was one such question. His reply is something like this: 'I am the writer of a story. The story has happened may be in my head. But it has happened. I am only reproducing the story on paper. I can't change the story. In the story, Shobha has decided to move on. She does not want to go back to Shankar. What can I do?'

At the June 2019 launch of the book *Gun Island*, Jnanpith Award-winning author Amitav Ghosh was in conversation with the movie director Shekar Kapur. Answering a question from the audience, Amitava echoed the same sentiment as Jayakanthan. He mentioned that characters had a life of their own and authors did not have control over them; they were not puppets to be pulled with a chain.

Almost a repeat of the same happened at the Tata Literature Live! Festival 2019 in Mumbai in a conversation between Shashi Tharoor and Alexander McCall Smith. Both have written multiple bestsellers. Answering a question, McCall Smith too opined that characters had their own lives and as he wrote he was often astounded at what happened to a character—characters died, some had severe depression and so on.

That made an impression. The novelist says that he cannot change the narrative. The characters have a life of their own. He is only writing the story. He has no power to change their motivations or actions.

I see this as a great way of distancing oneself from what one has created. We will explore this in future chapters as well, but those of us who get depressed when we face rejection make the mistake of confusing our persona with our story. If we can distance ourselves from what we presented, we can take a more sensible decision regarding rejection.

***What Was Rejected? Your Idea. Your CV. Your Story.
Not You.***

> **TAKEAWAY:** *Be ready to face rejection and don't let it destroy your self-belief. When faced with rejection, stop and think. Is it worth pursuing the same plan, the same path, or is it time to explore a less travelled path? Should you try out a new journey plan as a way of springing back?*

Facing Multiple Rejection Slips

Authors by the hundreds can tell you stories by the thousands of those rejection slips before they found a publisher who was willing to 'gamble' on an unknown.

—Zig Ziglar

The meeting was at IDBI Towers in Cuffe Parade, Mumbai. The chairman and managing director of IDBI, Mr M. Damodaran, had invited the team from IDBI Bank and other IDBI group companies to a meeting to discuss the new group identity that was being planned. Mr Damodaran introduced the team from the various IDBI entities to me and singled out a young executive saying he was among the brightest in the group, and added he was also, like me, an alumnus of IIM Calcutta. The meeting went well and all the parties involved thought the idea of integrating the identity of IDBI and IDBI Bank was in the right direction (the two merged a year or so later to become IDBI Bank).

A few months after that meeting, the said young executive called me and sought my inputs on what he called was his 'passion project'. I welcomed him to my office and we got talking. He said he had an idea for a book series and wanted to ask me for my inputs. He gave me a copy of his manuscript, and wanted me to read it at leisure. I thought the idea that was burning inside him was terrific and I put him in touch with a literary agent whom I knew. I lost track after that, till the book burst on to the scene some months later.

If you are wondering whom I am speaking about it is none other than Amish Tripathi, possibly India's best-known author and the creator of a new genre of writing, what is today called mythological fiction. Amish had spent many years in marketing before he started writing and did initially approach the idea of publishing his book in the usual tried-and-tested method of approaching publishers. But it is now well-known that all the publishers he approached rejected the idea of his book. They felt that the whole concept of 'mythological fiction' did not make any sense. Is it mythology? No. Is it fiction? Not really. Are the characters part of Indian mythology? Yes. But are their stories, tales as we have read elsewhere? No. Definitely not. So what was it?

Finally, Amish and his agent decided to publish the first book of the Shiva Trilogy, *Immortals of Meluha* themselves. And the book sold out instantly. Amish used his many years of marketing and consumer understanding to position the book in a unique space and built hype and hope around the book. Till I saw Amish's ad film on 'Legends of Meluha' I had never seen an ad, that too so well-produced, for an Indian fiction book. Or for any Indian book for that matter. Today, Amish is a much-awarded author, whose books have sold more than 3.5 million copies and counting. In September 2019, after his book *Raavan* hit the book stores, Amish created a new publishing record: his books occupied six of the top ten bestseller positions in India. Maybe that is a world record!

Amish got turned down several times. And interestingly, he is not the only bestselling (post facto) author to have faced this situation. Jeffery Archer was asked in an interview, 'Your first book *Not a Penny More, Not a Penny Less* was turned down by sixteen publishers, while J.K. Rowling's Harry Potter series was turned down by twelve publishers. What does it take for authors to win a publisher outright?' He replied in his own characteristic style and humour, 'Yes. We were (rejected many times). But I thought J.K. Rowling was turned down by eighteen publishers. It was twelve, was it? Well, I beat her then (laughs). Winning a publisher outright is just so difficult. They are getting 1,000 books a week. It is just so difficult and you need a bit of luck. In that sense, you need that someone who will read it and believe, "Oh here's something that is special."'

In the book *Resilence: Facing Down Rejection and Criticism on the Road to Success*, the author Mark McGuinness mentions the following authors whose work got rejected: Stephen King, William Faulkner, John le Carre, George Orwell, Sylvia Plath and Marcel Proust; and a list of twenty-five more.

If that does not tell you something about how tirelessly an author works to get his work published, here are a few more factoids.

J.K. Rowling was almost broke before she became the most famous author in the world. Speaking at Harvard's graduation ceremony, J.K. Rowling shared her rejection story: 'You might never fail on the scale I did. But it is impossible to live without failing at something, unless you live so cautiously that you might as well not have lived at all—in which case, you fail by default.' When Rowling was writing her first *Harry Potter* book, she was divorced, bankrupt and on welfare. Finally, when she found a publisher, she was told that she should get a proper job because there was no money in children's books. She is now a billionaire.

Today, Stephen King is hailed as an author who created a new blend of suspense, horror, mystery, supernatural and fantasy novel. But in 1973, when he was writing his first novel he was broke, lived in a trailer and drove a rundown car. His wife worked at Dunkin' Donuts and he taught English at a private high school to pay his bills. When he finished his first novel and sent it to thirty publishers, all of them turned it down. But King had a very supportive wife who in fact encouraged him to convert *Carrie*, which was a story she discovered in the trash bin, into a novel. *Carrie* was published in mid-1974 and started King's journey to the top of the heap. He has over sixty books to his credit and nineteen have been top-selling novels. Many of his books have been converted into high-grossing movies. And remember it all started with multiple rejections. And Stephen King says, 'Optimism is a perfectly legitimate response to failure.'

Jack Canfield, the author of the multi-million-copies-selling *Chicken Soup for the Soul* series, was rejected 144 times before a publisher stepped forward. When Canfield said he wanted to sell 1.5 million copies in eighteen months, the publisher laughed and said they'd be lucky if they sold 20,000. That first book sold 8 million copies in USA and 10 million across the world. Canfield says, when faced with rejection: 'So the reality is that you just have to say, "I am more committed to my vision than I am committed to your doubt or my fear", and just go for it.'

Ernest Hemingway was called a 'bombastic dipsomaniac' when he submitted *The Sun Also Rises*. George Orwell's *Animal*

Farm was rejected by T.S. Eliot. One editor declared that Vladimir Nabokov's *Lolita* should be 'buried under a stone for a thousand years'.

In the book *Hit Makers*, Derek Thomson, a senior editor at *The Atlantic* and a weekly news analyst for NPR (National Public Radio of USA) tells a story about a songwriter of Indian origin, Savan Harish Kotecha. Kotecha received 160 rejection letters while trying to break into the highly competitive music business. He eventually landed a job as a writer and producer for other singer/songwriters such as Madonna, Nick Jonas, Backstreet Boys, Ariana Grande, Usher, Justin Bieber and One Direction. Interestingly, Kotecha's journey to selling more than 200 million copies of his song started with rejection upon rejection upon rejection. Today, he has amassed many awards and multiple Grammy and Golden Globe nominations.

In India too, today's household names like Chetan Bhagat, Preeti Shenoy and Ashwin Sanghi have faced rejections. Anees Salim, my former colleague at FCB Ulka, who won the Sahitya Academy Award in 2018 and the Crossword Prize in 2015 for his novel *Blind Lady's Descendants* says he has not kept count of the rejections slips he has got.

In my own way, I too have had to face rejection on my writing journey.

My first attempt at writing was a book of advertising cases—*FCB Ulka Brand Building Advertising—Cases & Concepts I*. A well-meaning friend thought that there would be a ready market for a book of Indian advertising cases. To get a stronger endorsement, he sent the draft of the book to a friend of his who was an authority on Integrated Marketing Communication in a leading B-School in the US. Unfortunately, he got a rather sad reply from his friend: 'Sorry to disappoint, but I wonder which publisher would want to publish a collection of cases that read as if they are promotional pieces for the ad agency.' My friend was very crestfallen on getting this response and admitted so much in his mail to me. But that did not stop me from hunting for a publisher and eventually finding one in Tata McGraw Hill. The commissioning editor there, V. Deepa was willing to take a gamble and had the confidence that the book would be accepted in Indian business schools. Fortunately for her (and me), the book sold well and went into several reprints in due course.

If this is the case with books, films and television serials are no better. Even the most highly rated comedy serial *Seinfeld* (a show about nothing) did not almost see the light of day. The pilot was tested and did not do well. When it was aired once it got a tepid response. As is always the case, it took one gutsy production commissioning executive at NBC to stick his neck out for the programme. He decided to produce four episodes, reportedly the shortest first season for any serial in American television history, and *Seinfeld* became an urban legend.

In my book *Nawabs, Nudes, Noodles*, I have written about my encounter with Dilip Kumar (now known as A.R. Rehman) in 1990 when he was facing multiple rejections in the Tamil movie industry, and was even contemplating moving to Australia. He was then doing ad films and jingles as a way of keeping busy. But all that changed with the film *Roja* released just two years later, in 1992. Now of course, he is an Oscar winner with an awesome global reputation.

Even the Beatles were rejected by multiple record labels including Decca Records which said, 'Guitar groups are on the way out. The Beatles have no future in show business.' The Beatles did get signed up by a record label and they sold more singles in the UK than any other group in living memory. They have moved an amazing 177 million units in the USA, again more than any other group. And they were told they had 'no future'.

Why is it that rejection is such a common occurrence in the world of arts?

Books, film ideas, television pilots, music, theatre—all of them get a disproportionate share of rejections. But its creators do not tire. They do not give up. They do not get distracted. How come?

The two protagonists in these rejection tales come from two different starting points. The creator wants to do something different, something that has not been done before. The buyer or the approver comes from the place of results and thinks on these lines—this works, this sells, this is risky, this does not sell. And when they encounter something that they cannot put into a convenient pigeon hole, they reject. Well, to be fair, I am sure they are looking for fresh material, but the challenge is to understand the amount of difference they are willing to tolerate. College romance is working. Maybe workplace romance is the next hot trend. Mythologies from Mahabharata are working. What next, maybe something from the Ramayana or the Krishna Leela?

Let us switch tracks and see what we can learn from the pig-headedness of these famous authors, who continued to reach out to more and more publishers, till they got a 'yes'.

First is that they believed in what they created. It was not a flight of fantasy, unless of course, it was a fantasy novel. They had done enough reading, research and introspection, before they started writing. And most authors tend to write and rewrite many times. As a famous author commented, he wrote 2000 words a day when he was in the process of writing a new piece of fiction, and often he *rewrote* 1000 words every day before he wrote a fresh 1000 words. So it is truly a passion project. Alexander McCall Smith claims that he writes 1000 words an hour; often churning out 3000 to 4000 words a day. Every day.

Second, a creator is ready to take a 'no' for an answer. They know that what they have created will not win a nod from the first place. They are prepared to face rejection, and not get blown away. Anticipating and facing rejection is something that is par for course when you are embarking on a writing journey.

Finally, creators have the inner conviction to keep at it and not lose their self-confidence as they pile up rejection slips.

Creators of ideas, books, music, television serials and movies are today faced with yet another rejection dilemma. Your viewers may not like what you have created. For instance, the hit HBO show *Game of Thrones* (GOT) concluded with its eighth season in mid-2019. The fans were disappointed and they created a petition to HBO to remake it; more than 1.5 million signatures were garnered. George R.R. Martin, the author of the books on which the series was based, has spoken about the backlash (or rejection) the last season of the series has attracted. Martin has been outspoken about the 'toxic' culture of online fandoms and thinks it is making the whole process very volatile for artists to work in. He has said, 'The internet is toxic in a way that old fanzine culture and fandoms—comics fans, science fiction fans—in those days was not.' But taking cognisance of the comments, or maybe not, he has assured readers in his blog that the last volumes of his novels, yet to be published, won't be the same (as the last season of GOT). A tailpiece on the GOT final season brouhaha is that it went on to win twelve Emmy Awards, the highest number any programme won that year.

That was indeed an interesting twist to the rejection plot. Adoring fans rejected the last instalment and were so committed that they wanted the author to do it differently.

But are there valuable lessons to be learnt from these authors for most of us who are in regular corporate jobs?

Assume that you are a young copywriter in an ad agency. You get the brief and you work on your idea for a week and are ready to present the ideas to the creative director. He takes one look at the idea and shoots it down. You can retreat into a shell or go back to rework the job, polish it and present it again. Or do something else.

Here is what happened with a dear friend.

Paul Vinod is a very talented copywriter now based in New York. He started his career in Ulka Hyderabad. He moved to Ogilvy Bangalore to work on large brands and ended up working on Titan for many years. He recounted this story to me. The client had briefed the agency to work on a campaign for their new model, Titan Slim, the world's slimmest watch. Paul and his art partner had a great idea. They presented it to their boss, the regional creative director, who did not think much of it. But Paul knew it was a good idea and saved it for a rainy day. The worldwide creative director of Ogilvy, Neil French was in their office the following month on a routine visit. When he asked the teams to show him something that they believed in and that had not been presented to the client, or had been bombed by the client, Paul remembered the Titan Slim campaign that he had salted away in the bottom drawer. He pulled out the campaign and timidly showed it to Neil French. The response he got bowled him over: 'Wow, this is outstanding work. Has this been presented to the client?' Paul sheepishly admitted that his boss had 'bombed' aka 'rejected' the idea. Neil said this has to be presented and so the campaign which was really a large 'bar code' with one of the lines replaced with a super-slim Titan Slim watch was dusted up and presented to the client. It took Titan a few seconds to approve the campaign. The ad ran in all the leading print publications, went on to be rated as the most celebrated ad of the year, sold a ton of Titan Slim watches, and also garnered Paul and his team a lot of industry awards and recognition.

In creative businesses, good ideas can get rejected by the powers that be or by the client. The smart architects, the smart copywriters, the smart lyricists, the smart musicians always have a bottom drawer where they store the so-called 'rejected' ideas. Knowing fully well they will get a second chance to present the idea, may be to a different client. So if you think an idea is good, maybe you should save it for a rainy day.

**The question: Do you have a bottom drawer where you save
your 'rejected' ideas?**

Conviction in what you have done. The ability to not give up.
The tenacity to keep at it. And finally, not let the rejections
affect your inner worth. Those are the lessons all of us can learn
from the creative folks we met in this chapter.

Multiple rejections do not always mean that the road is
closed. There is always a small lane that can open up to take
you to your new destination.

TAKEAWAY: *Be ready to anticipate and accept rejection. If you
are convinced about what you are setting out to do, don't let
rejection derail you. If your heart says that you have a winning
concept, don't give up. Brush off the rejection and spring back to
make a fresh attempt.*

The Charm of Rookie Rejection

Take risks in your life. If you win, you can lead.
If you lose, you can guide.

—Swami Vivekananda

Have you ever felt that you are being set up to be rejected? To fail in the duty assigned to you. Why were you assigned that task in the first place? Weren't there better, more qualified people to handle this? Why you, when you were quite happy doing your regular job well?

Let me explain what I may be trying to imply. Your company wants to land a very important assignment from a very important customer. The whole team has worked hard to ensure that the final pitch presentation is perfect. As you are getting ready to do a trial presentation in your office, your boss says that you will be the first person to stand up and present to the customer group. You are very surprised and make polite noises that you have never done it. Your boss and the whole team say that you should stand up and present. They make more encouraging noises. And you get emboldened to take on the challenge.

Or let us think of a scenario of a troublesome assignment. Say, a very irate customer who needs to be handled. You want your superior to take the call from the customer. But he refuses. He knows it is a very important customer and a lot is riding on it. He insists that you should handle the tricky assignment by yourself. You leave his cabin wondering how this is going to pan out. Why did he push you into the deep end of the pool? Doesn't he know that you are mortally scared of depths? What happens if the customer rejects all your moves? *Are you being set up to be rejected?* Is the boss trying to protect his own backside by pushing you to the war front?

As a young brand manager at Boots Company, I was given the responsibility of handling the most important prescription brand in the company's portfolio: Brufen. The brand came with a lot of history. The molecule, Ibuprofen was a discovery of the pharmaceutical research laboratories of the UK company, Boots. In the '70s and '80s, Boots Company of UK had a retail arm (Boots The Chemist, which still exists in many parts of the world) and a pharmaceutical development and marketing arm. Interestingly, in India, they only had the pharmaceutical arm; this then became part of Knoll and later Abbott. Back to the Brufen story. The original drug Ibuprofen was indeed a big breakthrough and spurred numerous other drugs in the category called 'Non-Steroidal Anti-Inflammatory (NSAID)' drugs.

In an advertisement released in 2019 by the British government about the great discoveries that emanated from Great Britain, Ibuprofen found mention along with the discovery of 'gravity' and 'steam engine'. So clearly, Ibuprofen was a big deal. When I started handling the brand Brufen,

I had no knowledge of pharmaceutical marketing, having worked for three years in advertising, across multiple product categories, but not prescription medicine brands. So it was a steep learning curve for me and the environment that Boots provided for learning was indeed fantastic. I had a great set of colleagues who were more than eager to teach me the ropes and the bosses were all really supportive. I did manage to learn the ropes pretty quickly and even saw the launch of Brufen400 which became a runaway success. Today, Brufen is a small brand in the big booming Indian pharmaceutical market, but in the mid-1980s it was ranked among the top five pharmaceutical brands by the sales audit firm ORG. And I was proud that I played a small role in all this.

Then we had a shock.

The regional manager from South India called to say that there was a problem in Kerala. Apparently, the drug inspector in Kochi had seized stocks of Brufen under a 'mis-labelling' complaint. He had issued a stop-sales order with immediate effect. Brufen was a very important brand, and Kerala was a key market for them. So this news travelled very fast to and within the head office. The regional manager had also indicated that the said drug inspector was known for indulging in such practices and pharma companies had succumbed to his demands, after resisting for a few days. It was always a small violation and the penalty was always 'stop-sales'. The team in the head office was divided on what the company should do. The sales-oriented lot said that we should quickly find a way out of this. The other team said that we were not in the wrong. Our labelling requirements were all cleared by the drug controller of Maharashtra and everything was kosher. So we should fight back.

In this situation, the question was who should be sent to Kerala to handle the problem. The head of regulatory approvals? The head of the legal department? The person dealing with labelling? The head of sales? Or the young brand manager? You can guess how this cookie crumbled.

It was decided that I would have to make the hurried trip to Kochi the next day (mind you all the above happened between 10.30 a.m. and 4.30 p.m.). I did not know what to expect. Was I being sent as a 'sacrificial goat'? What were the chances that I could argue my case when the regional manager was saying that many other companies had fallen for this ruse? We quickly informed the depot manager at Kochi that I was coming the following day and that we would meet the drug inspector in his office at 10.30 a.m.

As I reached home, I remembered that my cousin who was based in a small town in Kerala, not too far from Kochi, was related through his wife, to one of the senior drug inspectors of Kerala. I was worried if I was going to be meeting him the next day. And if it was not him, I wanted to know from him what would be the best course of action for us to take. How should I fight? Should I push back? Or should I apologise and succumb?

There were no mobile phones those days, but I did have a company phone at home. I called my cousin, who responded that his brother-in-law was posted in Thrissur and was not in Kochi anymore. I told my cousin about my problem and he suggested that I should speak with his brother-in-law and take his views, before I headed to Kochi. Thanks to the miracle of STD, I managed to speak with my cousin's brother-in-law around 9 p.m. He gave me a patient hearing and said that this was the modus operandi of some of his colleagues, unfortunately. He suggested that I meet the said drug inspector and plead my case.

In his understanding, the labelling violation, if any, was not a very major one and a sales ban was a very extreme action. In effect, it sounded like the drug inspector was using a Patton Tank to kill a mosquito. But it was within his powers to give us time to make amends, and lift the ban. If the drug inspector refused, I needed to say that I was going to meet the regional drug controller in Thiruvananthapuram the next day and I had to keep repeating this ad nauseum.

Armed with all this additional dope, I boarded the flight with a little less fear of rejection. My regulatory team and legal team had armed me with a lot of paperwork about how we were fully compliant with the laws of the land. I was not sure what would happen, but was now a tad less nervous.

The flight landed on time and the depot manager and the regional manager were both there to update me. They were sceptical about my chances of solving such a 'big' problem. They too felt that I was being set up to fail. Rejection was guaranteed.

The depot manager had done his homework and told me that the same scam had been pulled on more than five companies in the last six months and all of them had gone on to settle with the very same drug inspector. He was pushing hard that we should not fight and should look at an amicable settlement. The regional manager who was losing sales by the minute concurred. I explained my late-night calls to them but they were not sure it would work though they also felt that if I could drop a hint that I knew people in the Kerala drug control department, it might work in our favour. No one was sure what to expect as we drove to the drug inspector's office.

The drug inspector was very polite and was happy that 'someone from Head Office' had flown down so quickly to meet with him. He did not show displeasure that I looked a youngster. Maybe my Malayalee-sounding name helped, though my knowledge of Malayalam did not. He explained the reason for the ban and said that we needed to amend the labelling information as soon as possible.

Those days the Central Drug Authorities had implemented a rule that the generic name of the drug ought to appear in a bigger font than the brand name. So 'Ibuprofen' had to appear bigger than 'Brufen'. Most companies complied with it by making the font taller. Boots had also done that, but he felt that Brufen was taller than the drug name 'Ibuprofen' by a millimetre or so. In his mind this was a 'big violation' which was harming the lives of millions. I argued that Brufen was a brand used by millions of patients across Kerala and many of them were using it for long-term treatment of chronic conditions like arthritis and back pain. There was no possibility of any harm being caused to them, at least as per all the research that was available with us. But he would not budge and insisted that we should make the change. Some suggestion of a settlement was made by one of the hangers-on, but we decided to ignore the comment. I repeated what I was told to say: 'We will approach the regional drug inspector in Trivandrum for relief.' I must have repeated this at least five times. I was then asked why I would take the trouble of going to Thiruvananthapuram, if things could be sorted out in Kochi itself? But we ignored this.

Since it was an impasse, we made some polite noises. I spoke warmly about my numerous trips to Kerala, my cousin who was a fairly well-known businessman in a neighbouring town and so on. I don't know if I mentioned my cousin's brother-in-law, but maybe I did. When we reached our office around 2 p.m. we were told that the drug inspector's office had called at least five times asking if we had got back (remember these were the days before mobile phones). They wanted us to get back to their office once again. We were not sure what to expect. Was he going to ban more brands of Boots (there goes my job, I thought)? Or was there a light at the end of the tunnel?

We rushed back to the drug inspector's office and as soon as we entered his office we realised that the scenario was very different. We could sense that something had changed. The drug inspector explained that we should have waited a bit in his office and should not have left in a hurry. He was going to make some suggestions for solving the problem. He said that he would visit the depot the following Monday and give an order lifting the ban on sales, with a proviso that we should get the labelling cleared with the Mumbai drug controller's office as soon as possible. I realised that something had worked. So I upped my game and insisted that I would go to Thirvananthapuram, if I did not get the relief letter forthwith. After hemming and hawing for a bit, the requisite letter was given to us. We had three months to sort out the problem.

My trip turned out to be a success. Against all odds.

We got back to the Kochi depot and I should admit that both the depot manager and the regional manager were very surprised at the sudden turn of events. Was my mention of going to Thiruvananthapuram the trigger? Or was my mentioning my cousin's name the trigger? I was not sure what worked, but something had worked and what was bound to be a sure-fire rejection, turned out to be a successful trip.

As I boarded the flight the next day, I wondered what had made my boss pick me for this dangerous trip. I could have faced rejection and failed miserably. I could have caused a bigger problem. I suppose I was picked because I was young and less hidebound in my thinking. My Kerala connections may have also had a role to play, but I am not sure. All told, I managed to find wiggle room and get out of a sure rejection situation.

A postscript to this story is that the team in Mumbai that dealt with the regulators found that the labelling was indeed a little erroneous, and the Kochi drug inspector was probably right in pointing this out.

Did you ever anticipate a 'sure rejection'?

Think back, have you been sent on such missions, where you felt that you had very little chance of success. What did you do before you headed out? Did you go with the feeling that you were going to get rejected and so you ended up not trying to turn things around? Or did the anticipation of a sure rejection get you to explore new avenues? Have you faced situations where you seemed to be ill-prepared to face the barrage of questions being thrown at you? Have you cursed your superiors for sending you to face the music, instead of facing it themselves?

In the book *Rookie Smarts*, Liz Wiseman speaks about the importance of the ability and willingness to learn over business experience. A rookie is someone who is new to a given role and not necessarily a fresh graduate or engineer. It could be a brand manager who has ten years of experience who is asked to clean up customer service. Wisemen feels this rookie is more likely to succeed if she embraces her curiosity by experimenting with new ideas, instead of falling back on years of 'best practices' embedded in the company. Rookies are great at learning from their mistakes, while the more experienced folks tend to hide their mistakes. Rookies are also willing to take inputs and ideas from the most unusual sources in their quest for knowledge. The veterans spend their time showing off how they know all that is to know.

I am sure you have come across situations where you were able to think of an out-of-the-box solution that your boss had not dreamt of.

Let me illustrate this with another example. I had joined UDI Yellow Pages as the Head of Sales in 1987 and we were setting up India's first professionally managed Yellow Pages operation in Mumbai, Delhi and Kolkata. It was a mammoth direct ad sales operation with a team numbering over 350. I had very little frontline sales experience but was given the task of heading the sales force as the GM-Sales. I had an American expat as my direct boss and he came with a lot of directory selling experience, and was a wonderful person to work with. Unfortunately, we had a rather tough chairman who was not satisfied with our progress after the initial eight-week period (we even had a harrowing meeting with him once, that lasted eight hours; we were not served even a cup of tea for the entire length of the meeting; possibly the worst workday of my life).

As I started looking at new avenues for generating sales, maybe an aftermath of the stressful time with the chairman, I wondered if we could get consumer goods brands to advertise in the Yellow Pages. My boss, the large American, was sure that it was a waste of time. He insisted that nowhere in the world did packaged consumer products like soap, toothpaste and shampoos advertise in the Yellow Pages. But he asked me to try. Anything for an extra dollar of sales was his philosophy (another gem from him—'There is no publicity like bad publicity.'). I was ready for rejection but wanted to give it a shot since I had access to many consumer product companies through my old networks.

The first port of call in Delhi was Nestle. My friend who was a brand manager in Nestle (now one of the most respected global leaders) dismissed the idea of advertising on the front or back cover of the Yellow Pages (they were priced really exorbitantly). But as I started asking him to advertise in specific sections of the Yellow Pages, why not Milkmaid in the 'Sweet Shops' page, or Cerelac in the 'Paediatricians' page? He had an idea. He said he was also looking after the newly-created division that handled bulk sales to restaurants and caterers. He wanted to know if they could advertise Nestle Food Services in a relevant page. I told him that we were getting good traction in the 'Marriage Services' page. So it was there that Nestle took a half-page ad, across all three cities where the UDI Yellow Pages were to be launched. It was my big breakthrough into the FMCG space.

Soon after, we brought Hindustan Lever and Colgate on board. So an idea that was pooh-poohed ended up being not so stupid after all.

Remember if you are the rookie in the team, be bold with your suggestions and hopefully you will end up doing something surprising and successful. If you are overseeing a team of bright young executives, you should not hesitate from letting them jump into the deep end. And expect them to fail more often than succeed. But also be ready for a miracle. Most importantly make sure that they are reassured all the time that the credit for the success will be theirs, but the failure will be your responsibility.

The next time you are chosen to take on a role where you feel you might get rejected, remember that you have been selected because you are supposed to have the 'Rookie Smarts'. So don't approach the situation like a veteran. Anticipate rejection. And use your creativity and innovation to see how you can make that sure-fire rejection into a success, with the understanding that your superiors will not punish you if you fail. And even if fail, you lose nothing. Try and spring in new directions.

> **TAKEAWAY:** *Never despair even if the task assigned to you has a high chance of rejection. Don't curse your luck, but use the fear of failure to explore new avenues and untested approaches. You may well be the recipient of 'Rookie Luck'.*

The Thin Audience Rejection Story

You get used to rejection and you don't take it personally.
—Daniel Craig

I must be one of the few people in the world who listens to Carnatic music while performing my exercise routine in the gym. Surrounded by much younger gym enthusiasts, I often wonder what would be their reaction if they find out what I am listening to, and successfully drowning out the loud pulsating gym music which seems to be the set piece in every gym. As I start writing this chapter, I can still hear the song *Yaaro Ivar Yaaro* (Who is this person), a one-hour-long musical odyssey rendered exquisitely by the Carnatic music virtuoso Sanjay Subrahmanyan. The song rendered in Raga Bhairavi (the Carnatic raga and not the same as Raag Bhairavi in Hindustani), presents Rama's first sighting of Sita, as he walks past her palace balcony. 'Who can it be? What is her name? In this beautiful Mithila which abounds with clouds and wealth, who is this who stands in front of the ladies quarters?' goes the wonderful song.

Sanjay Subrahmanyan is one of the, if not the most popular Carnatic music singers in India. A chartered accountant by qualification, he decided to pursue a career in music well in his twenties. So he is not a childhood genius. In a programme held for raising funds for the health insurance of retired school teachers of his alma mater, Vidya Mandir High School in Chennai, he admitted that the first time he performed on stage was in his tenth grade for a school function. And the teacher, Miss Kanaka asked him, before he went on stage, '*Dai Sanjay, Vatapi Nalla Paduvayilla?*' (Hey Sanjay, hope you can sing the song 'Vatapi' well?). He fondly remembered the incident and reaffirmed that he was ready to perform pro-bono for his school anytime.

Sanjay was recognised in the year 2015 by the Music Academy of Madras with its highest honour, 'Sangeeta Kalanidhi'. Apparently, only two people in the entire history of the Music Academy, which is an eighty-nine-year-old institution, have received the award at an age of less than fifty. Obviously, the Academy recognises artists after they have achieved a level of excellence and held on to that level for excellence not just for years, but for decades. So a flash in the pan, a great song, a wonderful album may get you an award, a Grammy even, but to get the Sangeeta Kalanidhi, you need to perform at a high level for decades. Now if you juxtapose the fact that Sanjay started his serious musical career only in his twenties and he was recognised by the Music Academy when he was forty-seven, it speaks volumes about his rise, his discipline and dedication. In his acceptance speech, he mentions that he has many people to thank but also pointed out that he does not perform a song on stage unless he has practised it fifty times at home.

What is so great about singing a song you may ask. During the Carnatic music season in Chennai, which lasts for almost fifteen days, from 15 December to 1 January, Sanjay often performs every day. And no song is ever repeated. An average concert involves ten to fifteen songs. Many songs he would be performing for the first time on stage. Do the math on how much he must be working behind the scene before he goes on stage. I am not saying that other musicians do not put in this kind of effort. They probably do. But possibly, before every concert, he puts in a lot more preparation as an individual musician. He does not refer to any paper, notebook, smart phone or iPad when on stage like most Carnatic singers/ musicians do. Amazingly, he does not even take a sip of water while performing. So his concerts are a great demonstration of his prowess in singing and also his physical strength and self-discipline.

The *Outlook* magazine in its 31 December 2018 issue had this to say about the wild fan following of Sanjay Subrahmanyan: 'They filter in half an hour before Sanjay Subrahmanyan's fourth concert of the December music season at Brahma Gana Sabha. Exchange pleasantries and enquire if the others have reached … You can't see them in the darkness but feel their enthusiasm—their love of music and of the fifty-year-old vocalist, a Carnatic music superstar… This is *Sanjay Bhaktha Jana Sabha*, a fan group.' (Pretty much like the fan groups of rockstars).

What has all this got to do with the topic of rejection, you are probably wondering. Stay with me for a bit. The story is just beginning.

On 1 January 2019, my wife Nithya, my friend Balu and I were fortunate to get tickets for Sanjay's New Year concert in Chennai. The concert was advertised as a four-hour marathon and tickets were sold out weeks before the date of the concert. The 1000 seats in the hall were all full. In Carnatic concerts, there is the peculiar custom of allowing *rasikas* (music-lovers) to sit on the stage with the artiste. The stage was also packed. My good friend Ravi, in spite of his strong connections in Chennai had to sit out. As always Sanjay's concert was out of this world. And as always, there was almost a ten-minute standing ovation at the end of the concert.

You get the picture. Sanjay is the superstar of Carnatic music.

But the next story will tell you a bit more about the mettle of the man.

First Edition Arts organises interesting musical events in Mumbai. They attempt to curate music in interesting styles and venues. For example, they organise Carnatic music concerts in not-so-traditional settings. They explain that they want to take the classical arts to new areas of the city. In addition to organising great concerts they also do a wonderful job of video recording the concerts, with multiple cameras and great sound engineering (you can check out the First Edition Arts Channel on YouTube).

We were delighted to hear that First Edition Arts was organising a concert of Sanjay Subrahmanyan in Mumbai, where I live. The venue was also great, St Andrews Auditorium in Bandra. The auditorium is attached to the St Andrews College and has been host to numerous jazz and rock concerts as well as wonderful musical shows like *Jesus Christ Superstar* and English plays. So it was a strange venue to host a dyed-in-the-wool Carnatic concert. As always, we had booked our tickets early and landed up well before the start of the show.

When we reached the venue, we were probably the first to arrive. It was a double bill with a Hindustani concert before Sanjay was to perform. The Hindustani concert was very thinly attended, and we attributed it to the fact that it was a young Sarod artiste performing. We waited and waited for the fans of Sanjay to show up. By the way, his shows in Shanmukhananda Auditorium in Sion are always packed (Shanmukhananda is possibly the biggest auditorium in Mumbai with a capacity of 2700 plus). The first concert was over. The hall was cleared for sound checking by Sanjay and team. Then the first bell sounded. Then the second. Then the third. The auditorium door opened. And we found that we were among the fifty people who had gathered to listen to the maestro. I was shocked. I managed to catch hold of one of the key moving forces behind First Edition Arts to find out what had happened. I was also worried that Sanjay should not get a wrong impression about his fans in Mumbai; he makes at least one trip to Mumbai, sometimes two every year. We did not want him to put Mumbai in his 'no-fly zone'.

What the organisers told me blew me away. They said that they had met Sanjay backstage to explain the fiasco. The unusual choice of venue in Bandra, the bad traffic, the working day etc. had worked against the hall filling up. They sincerely apologised to Sanjay for the 'rejection of a thin audience'. I am told his response went something like this: 'You have invited me to perform and I will perform. Don't worry if there are only ten people in the audience. I will perform for those ten people.'

The concert started as promised at 7 p.m. and Sanjay performed for full three hours. It was a fabulous concert, one of his best ever, I think. The audience were spellbound, some listening to Carnatic music for the first time. As always there was a standing ovation at the end. Since there were not too many in the audience, some of us in the audience could actually go up on stage to thank Sanjay for the wonderful performance. Which he gratefully acknowledged.

While the concert did not get a full house, the famous writer, journalist and art critic Shanta Gokhale was in the audience. And here is what she said in the *Mumbai Mirror* of 2 November 2017: 'Attending on Saturday, I heard young sarodist Abhishek Borkar play with deep involvement but to a sadly sparse audience. The numbers increased for Sanjay Subrahmanyan who followed, but only to some extent. It was shocking that this part of Mumbai (the concert was held in St Andrews) could not muster enough people to even half fill the hall for one of the leading stars of Carnatic music. I do not exaggerate when I say that Subrahmanyan, recently awarded the prestigious title of Sangita Kalanidhi, was like one of those giant fireworks packed with gunpowder and tube of metal salts and oxides that burst into the sky and send down showers of stars in a breathtaking display of light, colour and form… He sang for a full three hours and, had practical considerations not intervened, could have gone on longer given the freshness of musical ideas that kept pouring out of him. Unfortunately, being only superficially acquainted with the Carnatic system, I can only speak here of things that blew my laywoman's mind away that evening.'

I could not have said it better, though my knowledge of Carnatic music is a tad better than Shanta Gokhale's.

There was a lesson in this for me, definitely.

What does it take for a top artiste to face an almost empty auditorium, yet perform to his top potential, with the same energy and enthusiasm?

What can we learn from this? About commitment? About dedication? About managing our ego?

Books are full of stories of today's musical and movie icons facing rejection early in their career.

Meryl Streep was a twenty-six-year-old, with a good acting reputation, when she auditioned for a role in the movie *King Kong*. She did not hear back from the company; the standard response when you are rejected. Apparently, the famous producer Dino De Laurentis Sr rejected her saying 'Che Brutta' to his team (that loosely means 'Ugly' in Italian). Meryl Streep, who to his surprise knew Italian, quickly answered back '… this is it. This is what you get.' Recounting this rejection Meryl Streep in *The Graham Norton Show* said, 'I'm sorry that I'm not beautiful enough to be in … *King Kong*.' Well, she has probably won more Academy Awards than any other actor in history. But she was rejected for the female lead role where the hero was a 1000-pound gorilla.

Walt Disney was fired from one of his first jobs as an animator from Kansas City Star in 1919. He was fired because he ostensibly lacked imagination and had no good ideas. Disney's next attempt Laugh-O-Gram studios went belly-up in 1923, before any of his cartoons were aired. Disney did not give up his dream. He moved to Hollywood and set up Disney Brothers (with his brother), which later became the Walt Disney Company, which continues to be one of the best know names in entertainment.

Walt Disney once said, 'All our dreams can come true—if we have the courage to pursue them.' So true.

Karan Johar is possibly one of the biggest producer directors in Bollywood. But as *Mumbai Mirror* (20 January 2020) reported, even Karan Johar was least prepared to receive negative reviews of what he thought was his grand magnum opus, *Kabhi Khushi Kabhie Gham* (K3G). He is reported to have admitted in a show, 'I thought I am making the biggest film in Hindi cinema since *Mughul-e-Azam….*' But the film, a big, big multi-starrer, did badly in term of reviews and awards, leading him to comment, 'K3G is the single biggest slap on my face and my biggest reality check'.

Rejection can attack us from anywhere.
Early in our career or later.

And rejection can be in various forms. Getting fired because your work is not appreciated. No call back from a casting agent. Or a very thin attendance at a much-touted show.

I have been invited to deliver talks at business schools and industry seminars. Some of them attract a full house. Some of them are where I face a half-empty auditorium. Once I accept the invitation, I do a sincere job of preparing on the given topic. The size of the audience is of secondary importance. At a recent industry event, a fellow panellist wryly commented that if the speakers on the various panels (current and yet-to-go-on-stage) left the hall, the hall would be empty. But an almost empty hall should not make you feel rejected, is the lesson. Also when you go out to perform, you cannot allow your own commitment to your chosen art form be dependent on the size of the audience.

Now think back. Have you got upset that the intended audience was not there to meet you? Here is a scenario. You have been invited to make a presentation about your new idea to a VC firm. You land up there and find that of the ten people who were to attend the presentation, six are missing. What does that do to you? Do you feel rejected? Do you show your displeasure? Do you cut short your talk/presentation?

What you don't know is that in that audience of six there may be someone who has a powerful voice. Someone like Shanta Gokhale, who can take your story to the bigger world out there.

My own interpretation of the situation goes something like this: you have been invited and you have done your full preparation for the presentation. If you are fully ready, you should not worry about the size of the audience or their credentials. You should assume that the most important people are in the conference room and perform with full gusto.

Remember, a thin audience does not reject you. They are there to appreciate your performance. You will be doing a disservice to your responsibility and professionalism, if you reject the thin audience. You should embrace them as if they are the most important people in the world and give out your best.

Karma will find a way to repay you, perhaps with a glorious review in a leading paper the next Monday. Perhaps in some other shape or form.

> **TAKEAWAY:** *Anticipate a not-so-perfect audience. And don't let the absence of a key person or the right audience dampen your enthusiasm. Perform as if you are facing a full house. And you may very well get an unexpected gift.*

The Hot Rejection Envelopes

Our greatest glory is not in never failing,
but in rising every time we fail.

—Confucius

Everyone seems to know what happens to you when you are hit by a rejection. There is an old saying that goes, 'The Postman Always Rings Twice' (it also became a blockbuster 1981 movie starring Jack Nicholson and Jessica Lange.)* In IIT Madras however, the postmen knew when to ring twice and when not to ring at all.

When I was a student there, the early part of every year was exciting, especially if you were in the final year of your BTech programme. Some were busy writing the GRE, to apply to international universities. Others were doing some preparation to take the CAT to try their hand at getting into an IIM. Today, all these applications and their responses happen via email. But in the late 1970s and 1980s, you were dependent

---

*In the old day, telegrams were expensive and usually the bringers of bad news. So a postman knocking (later, ringing) twice signalled trouble was on the way.

on the Indian Postal Service for applying and for getting your response. If you were applying to a university abroad it was an elaborate process of getting the dollar draft, the application, the very important recommendation letters and more put into an envelope and sent to multiple US universities. Then one waited for the response. Who brought the response? The trustworthy postman.

Postmen had their own way of handling the responses. Over time they understood which letter bearing an international stamp and an international university envelope was an 'acceptance' letter, and which was a 'rejection' letter. I am told the 'Dear John' or 'rejection' letters are often thin with just one page saying that you are not being considered for the Masters or PhD programme. In contrast, the acceptance letter often contains multiple forms to be filled out (I20, aid-seeking forms etc.). So the acceptance letters were bulky.

What do you think the postmen did?

One letter was going to evoke a sense of joy. Of happiness.

The other letter was going to evoke a sense of loss, a sense of rejection.

Postmen had a way of handling this. If they saw that the letter was thin, read rejection, they slipped it under your door, if your door was locked. Or even if your door wasn't locked. But if the letter was bulky, the postman left a slip saying that one had to meet him in the post office.

By handing over a bulky envelope, they got to congratulate the lucky student and also get a nice tip for their troubles. But more importantly, why were they slipping the rejection letter under the door? Was it because they did not want to be associated with the rejection letter and be the harbringer of bad news?

*Do all of us know how to anticipate and react to rejection?
Or do some of us have a thicker skin?*

Does this have something to do with our own upbringing and cultural and social milieu?

A dear friend was the head of marketing at one of India's biggest MNC consumer product companies. Given his successful track record, the company posted him to Japan where he served for almost five years as head of marketing before being promoted to head the operations of the same company in one of the larger African countries. He later returned to India and was the CEO of a large Indian consumer products company. I once asked him about the difference in handling teams in India vis-a-vis Japan and Nigeria.

He had an interesting story to tell and it hinged on how people reacted to rejection. When he moved from Japan to Nigeria, he found the going tough. His weekly meetings used to produce limited change in behaviour and actions from his new team. After seeing him struggle for over a month, a wise old office assistant approached him with some sage advice. The old man asked my friend, 'How do you give instructions to the team here?'; and my friend explained that he would normally end the meeting requesting the team for a status report on action taken. And nothing would happen. The old man asked, 'Why are you requesting action?'; my friend replied that he had spent five years in Japan, the only country other than India where he had worked, and that was what worked there. To which the old man said that in Nigeria you need to be a lot more stronger in your approach. People here are used to a more assertive way of being managed. Simple polite threats of rejection have no effect. The light bulb got switched on. And my friend decided to be a lot stronger with his threats of 'rejection' and work started happening superfast.

Culturally, the Japanese are very sensitive to rejection and so you only had to drop a hint—'This report can do with some improvement' or something on those lines; that was treated as a command for a complete rework. If you give the same instructions to your Indian team, chances are that they will make some layout changes and resubmit the very same report. Nigeria, I suppose is not very different. Even in India how a North Indian reacts to a rejection is often quite different from the way a typical South Indian reacts to the same rejection. So as you face rejection, do try to understand if there is a cultural paradigm at work in your way of handling the rejection.

In the article 'Find the Coaching in Criticism' in the *Harvard Business Review*, Prof. Sheila Heen and Douglas Stone point out the importance of knowing our own tendencies, of how we take feedback and rejection. Do we defend our action with facts, or do we argue with the other person on how they delivered the rejection, or do we strike back saying that it was unfair?

How do we react to rejection as time goes by? Do we allow the rejection to grow as time goes by or do we balance it with other inputs? Do we sleep on it only to wake up with a clearer head and a better way of understanding the rejection?

This takes us to a fundamental question:

Why is it that we fear rejection?

Guy Winch has written some very interesting stuff about rejection and his TEDx video (*Emotional First Aid*) is a must-watch if you want to understand the physiology and psychology of rejection. Let me try and present some interesting nuggets here.

As we saw earlier, neuroscientists have found that rejection piggybacks on physical pain pathways in the brain. If you map your brain activity when you are slapped by your mother, and compare it with the time when your dad firmly rejected your request for a new cycle, you will find that the parts of the brain that get lit up are similar. So rejection, though not physical, gets your brain to react the same way it reacts to a physical blow. It does not see the difference.

Painkillers actually reduce the emotional pain of rejection

Sounds absurd, doesn't it? But in lab experiments reported by Guy Winch in his engaging article '10 Surprising Facts about Rejection' (*Psychology Today*, November 2015) researchers gave a matched sample of two group of participants' painful rejection experiences. One group got a painkiller, the other lot got a sugar pill. The group that got a real painkiller reported significantly lesser emotional pain. So the next time, an analgesic tablet could be a useful way to reduce your own pain from a rejection.

There is a new science that is trying to understand how our psychology has been shaped over the millennia. These scientists go by the title 'Evolutionary Psychologists'. They study how our psychological responses may have got hardwired during the phase when we were all hunters and gatherers. In the prehistoric world full of wild animals, our only way of survival was through staying close to our tribe. So when our tribe rejected us, it was as good as a death warrant. Therefore, we dread being rejected by the group we belong to.

Apparently, we relive the emotional pain of rejection more vividly than physical pain. So the slap from your mom may be soon forgotten, but the rejection from your dad, or from your bunch of friends who did not include you in their team, is going to be remembered for long. Maybe even longer than the memory of the physical pain.

Stop for a moment now. What is the painful experience you have from your childhood? Was it your teacher slapping you? And what was the most cruel rejection experience you can recall? The fact that you were only made the twelfth man of the cricket team? Which was more painful then, and now?

Rejection upsets our 'need to belong' gene. So when we are rejected by one group or one company, it is important to reconnect with those who we love us. It is told that reaching out to those who care for us, in our moment of rejection is indeed a great salve to ease the pain of rejection. We will dig deeper into this as we look at how to process and recover from rejection.

What does rejection do to us? It makes us angry and aggressive. Research in the US has shown that rejection meted out to an adolescent can lead to violence, drugs, poverty and gang membership. Young Raghav (name changed) could not clear his Class X exams, while the rest of his class managed to get through. This led to him joining a gang of vagabonds. They spent time on Mumbai's Worli Sea Face every day. On a fateful day, the gang members dared Raghav to do a stunt on the sea face. They had to fish his body out a few hours later.

So not only does rejection lead to aggression and anger, it could also send us on a mission to destroy our self-worth. We bemoan our own self-worth, and our self-esteem is turned into pulp.

Research has also shown that rejection makes us dumb. Yes, it lowers our IQ. This has been proven through lab experiments again. Someone who has gone through a recent rejection ends up scoring significantly lower in IQ tests, tests of short-term memory and tests of decision-making.

When rejected, even by a somewhat inconsequential group, the hurt stays. Reasoning it out does not always work.

We feel the rejection a lot longer than we want to remember

So there are so many issues that are caused by rejection. Is there no remedy? Yes, there is.

Psychologists point out that we should try and address every aspect of the psychological wound that the rejection may have caused.

We need to soothe our emotional pain, protect our self-worth, be aware of our aggression and reach out to people to ease our fear of not belonging.

Guy Winch's book *Emotional First Aid—Healing Rejection, Guilt, Failure, and Other Everyday Hurts* and TEDx video speak about seven steps:

- Pay attention to emotional pain—recognise it when it happens and work to treat it before it feels all-encompassing.
- Redirect your gut reaction when you fail. (Remember that what is being rejected is not 'you'.)
- Monitor and protect your self-esteem—When you

feel like putting yourself down, take a moment to be compassionate to yourself.

- When negative thoughts are taking over, disrupt them with positive distraction.
- Find meaning in loss. (Is there something that you can learn from the loss?)
- Don't let excessive guilt linger.
- Learn what treatments for emotional wounds are effective for you (When down, what will help? A word with a mentor? Something else?)

In an engaging blog post, 'Rejection—A Loser's Guide—Physiologically, neurologically, anthropologically speaking rejection sucks', Adoree Durayappah-Harrison points us towards some other research that paints a gloomy picture about how rejection can really addle our brain. Scientists from University of Amsterdam found that unexpected social rejection is often associated with a significant response from our parasympathetic nervous system. When we swim our body adjusts our heart rate to pump harder so that we are able to move our hands, legs and neck/face, to breathe in and out. What happens to our heartbeat when we get a rejection message? Our heart rate drops and it takes a while for it to come back to normal.

If that is not bad enough, at Stony Brook University, researchers found that the area of the brain that gets active during the pain and anguish experienced during a social rejection, is the same part that is associated with motivation, reward and cravings. So is getting over a social rejection as difficult as getting over cocaine addiction, is the question posed.

Behavioural Economics is an emerging area of study and one of its leading proponents is psychologist Daniel Kahneman who received the Nobel Prize (Economics) in 2002 for his work on 'prospect theory'. The theory speaks about how people make choices in situations where they have to deal with risk. The concept of 'loss aversion' came out of this work. We feel the loss of Rs 1000 more than the joy of receiving Rs 1000. Thus we tend to be averse to losses, while not being motivated to potential gains. Small investors lose in the stock market since they are averse to booking a loss. They tend to believe that the stock they are holding will one day go up in value, little realising that an alternate investment may go up by a bigger amount.

After facing a rejection we tend to become more gloomy in our outlook and become more risk averse. This is called learned helplessness. We learn to behave in a helpless fashion. There is a famous experiment involving six monkeys in a cage, with a bunch of bananas hanging from the top. If the monkeys learn to climb one on top of another, they can get to the bananas. But the problem is that when they climb up and reach the bananas, there is a huge jet of water that hits them. So they try a few times and then give up. Experimenters then remove one monkey and replace it with a new monkey. Now this monkey tries climbing on top of another to reach the bananas. The five old monkeys, who have experienced the jet of water, quickly pull him down (no water is needed this time). As the experiment progresses, slowly, every one of the six old monkeys are replaced with new ones, but they never try to climb. They have learned that climbing up causes a lot of havoc, though they have never seen it.

Rejection also leads to an interesting phenomenon called 'catastrophising', says Durayappah-Harrison. It simply means that you tend to blow up a small rejection into a monumental one. For example, your request for transfer into a different department is pending. You don't know if it will be accepted or rejected. If you are 'catastrophising' you will build the scenario into multiple disasters: my request will be rejected; my current boss is going to be very upset with me; he is going to evaluate me poorly at the next appraisal; he may even give me a bad assignment; this may cause more stress at home and work; my wife may get upset with me for working so late every day; she may ask me to change my job; will I get a good enough job?

Think back about your own habits. Do you blow up rejections into 'catastrophes'? Are you inadvertently 'catastrophising'?

The remedy for rejection seems to be our ability to anticipate it and be ready to face it. And to tell ourselves that we can act and make it better.

Well the postmen of IIT probably knew all this and more, intuitively, when they delivered those letters. I even saw postmen speaking with students and counselling them with the advice that some students got many slim envelopes before they got a bulky one. Chin up, folks. The Postman Will Ring Twice. When the envelope is the right one.

> **TAKEAWAY:** *Be aware how you react to a rejection. Don't let the rejection push you into a negative spiral. Remember you have a spring inside you. Unleash its power to get you to a better place.*

Don't Take It Personally

Refuse to let the fear of rejection hold you back.
Remember, rejection is never personal.

—Brian Tracy

Life in this small village in Kerala was very enjoyable. Playing with friends. A dip in the village pond. School that did not tax you much. But for this young lad, it turned out to be a monotonous life. And given the fact that he had more than seven siblings and limited ancestral resources, he knew his calling was not a mundane village life. He had heard of an uncle who had set up business in the distant town of 'Madrasi' (or Madras, today's Chennai). So Madras it was. He landed up in that burgeoning city with just a small bag looking for a job in his uncle's little canteen, or should I glorify it and call it a café. He was assigned the job of cleaning tables and utensils first. He graduated to the job of grinding rice for idly and dosa. He realised that there was a fortune to be made in the café business. The city was full of wandering travellers, looking for simple, economical snacks and an occasional meal.

Our young man decided to go back to his village, sell his share of the family land and plunge into the business of setting up a vegetarian restaurant. He stumbled upon a great location near the Madras Central Station, and quickly took that little property on rent. It was a small business. In the early days, he did pretty much everything. From buying vegetables at the Kothavalchavadi wholesale market, to grinding dosa batter, to waiting on tables and then on the 'galla' (cash counter). His memory for people and dates, his excellent skills at arithmetic, and his ability to put his nose to the grinding stone, in this case literally, made him a very intuitive and successful businessman.

Those were the 1940s, heady days with the breeze of freedom flowing through the land. He saw freedom fighters march past his restaurant, heading to meetings at nearby grounds. Some of them did not have money to pay for their meal. He saw struggling theatre actors, including M.G. Ramachandran (MGR later became the Chief Minister of Tamil Nadu) and his brother M.G. Chakrapani walk in for a meal, and then discovering they had run out of cash.

Business was good. His little restaurant expanded and came to occupy one more building on Wall Tax road, next to the Madras Central Station (you could see platform no. 1 from the restaurant). He also built a meals section at a nearby location along the same arterial road. An affordable lodging house too was added. The little business developed a reputation for tasty food, affordable charges and clean rooms. The young man was no longer young. He had got married, had three children and grandchildren too. He realised that he had made a good life for himself and felt that he was obliged to do something in return for the city of Madras, that had given him so much. So one fine day in early 1960s he decided that he would hand over his beautiful spacious house located in the heart of the city to the Corporation of Madras, to be used as a Maternity Home and Child Care Centre. The Corporation was delighted to receive a large parcel of land and a good building, in a superb locality, for free. The Chief Minister of the state of Madras (now Tamil Nadu) was himself present at the handing-over ceremony.

As a sign of recognition, the government wanted to do something in return. No, unfortunately he did not get an award. But he was told that the Prime Minister of India was going to be visiting Madras and would be heading to address a public meeting near Madras Central Station. The philanthropist, if I can call him one, was informed that the Prime Minister's cavalcade would stop in front of his restaurant and he could greet the Prime Minster and hand over a bouquet to him. This was indeed a rare recognition. It was totally out of the blue. And it created a huge buzz of excitement in the family, among the restaurant staff, and among all the other small business folks in that area.

On that day, all along Wall Tax Road there were people gathered to catch a glimpse of the Prime Minister. In front of the restaurant was gathered the family of the businessman and his staff, ready with garlands and bouquets. The car was a white, open-top sedan, escorted by multiple vehicles and cops on motorcycles. As the cavalcade approached, there was palpable excitement all around. But all that ended in a fizzle. The car did not stop at the restaurant. No one knows what happened. But the car and the entire entourage just whizzed past.

How do I know all this? Well, I was then a six-year-old clutching the fingers of my cousin Ramjee, standing behind my grandfather who was the businessman who had got slighted.

This was a rejection of Himalayan proportions. More than fifty years later, I still have clear memories of what happened. And what happened next.

My uncle who was an up and coming lawyer in Madras High Court, and an author of several books, was more than agitated. A few of his friends too agreed with him. Their reasoning went as follows: we had not asked for the honour; the government offered it to us without any request from our side but did not stand by their commitment; this was like a slap on our face.

I remember a smart photographer telling my dad that he could create a picture by manipulating a photo of my grandfather holding a garland and a picture of the Prime Minister. Those were the days before computers and photoshop, if you were wondering why it was such an innovative suggestion.

Through all this fog and din, I could observe my grandfather soaking in the rejection. It was almost a textbook definition of what to do when you are rejected.

My grandfather did not get into a rage and start complaining about the shoddy treatment he received. He did not lash out at anyone. When someone suggested that we rush to the public meeting venue to seek an audience, he 'ssshhed' them and said we would not go anywhere. I now realise that he was practising what experts say we should do when hit by a rejection.

Don't take it personally

The fact the cavalcade did not stop could be for many reasons. If one wanted to complain, then thoughts on the lines of 'I didn't deserve the honour', 'I am nothing but a petty businessman', 'I should not have got my expectations so high' would have been the order of the day. A deep sulk or a mad rage might have followed.

I did not see any of that. There was almost a 'karmic' reaction to the whole incident. I remember my grandfather saying, 'Maybe they were running out of time. Or maybe they had a more important stop to make. Or maybe they mixed up the location.'

All of you would have heard of love at first sight. There is magic in the first sight and something happens. You realise that this person is the right person for you. Flip that around. What is your first reaction to a rejection?

Psychologists who study rejection say that your first reaction to rejection is indicative of how you will end up handling it. So while there are many prescriptions of how to handle rejection, the seven steps, the ten ways and so on, I noticed that most of these lists start with this simple advice: don't take it personally.

This got me thinking, what does it mean—'*Don't take it personally.*'

Imagine you have appeared for an important interview. And you were told that by the end of the day you would be told if you make it or not. You hear at 6 p.m. that you did not land the job. It is personal, isn't it? You were rejected or found inadequate for the job. What does it mean that you should not take it personally?

Let us play this scenario out. Maybe there were other candidates who were more suitable for this assignment. So they got the job. Maybe the company found you too highly qualified for the job, so they did not want to put a square peg in a round hole.

There is also the possibility that the person who was interviewing you was having a bad day. Maybe he was having personal issues to handle and was distracted. And he was not focused when he was interviewing you. Something you said switched him off. Maybe that was the end of your interview.

I have been in some situations where the candidate was perfectly fine, but the interviewing panel suddenly wanted to close the process and head out for a drink. The opposite has also happened. I remember interviewing young Harpreet Singh (name changed) in the small office of our headhunter in Nehru Place for a Territory Manager's job in UDI Yellow Pages Delhi. It was past 7.30 p.m. After going through ten, or was it fifteen, interviews through the day, my colleague Arvind Wable and I did not want to meet one more person who was keen on working in a hardcore sales supervisor's job. So we decided to give Harpreet exactly ten minutes (anything less would not have been fair to a person who had been waiting, dressed up if you please in a white shirt and tie, for more than four hours, to appear in the interview). But to our surprise in walks Harpreet at 7.30 p.m. full of beans. He lit up the room with his charm and energy. The ten-minute interview turned out to be a sixty-minute one. And he got the job.

On the face of it, Harpreet was all set for rejection. His interview was slotted at the end of a long day. The panel was tired as hell. But to his good luck, he did not let the time or the mood of the panel or the lighting in the room come in his way. He managed to make lady luck appear from behind the dark clouds to make his day.

You may not be so lucky. You may show some sign of tiredness. You may not bubble with enthusiasm at 7.30 p.m., after waiting for four hours. And you may miss making a good impression.

By not taking the rejection personally, you are getting ready to ride on the road to self-improvement and self-discovery.

It is probably easy to take the rejection personally.

For a minute discard your thoughts of not being deserving enough or having made mistakes. They are to be delved into. But not at the moment you get hit by rejection. When you get the rejection news, distance it from yourself.

Don't take it personally

Most definitely you should grieve your rejection. You should not bottle up the emotion, but you should not allow it to send you into deep depression. You should let the emotion flow over you.

By not making it personal, you are distancing the scar that it may cause you.

Play this scenario out. You have slogged for many days in putting together a project report and on the big day you present it to the Board. The Board gives you a patient listening, but rejects your proposal.

How will you react? Let me give you two versions.

The project has been rejected. It was my pet project. I had slogged for months on the project. I had put in all my knowledge and skills into shaping the project. I had used my vast network to do a deep analysis on the subject. I am devastated. The Board has rejected my proposal. My competence has been questioned. Am I not fit for the job? Am I to quit? Is my education and experience only worth this much? What should I do? Quit? Jump off the building?

Now the second version.

My project has been rejected. I did spend a lot of time on the project. I thought I had collected a lot of useful information in the process of developing the project. I learnt so many new things while working on the project. But it got rejected. Maybe the Board has other projects to look at. Maybe they are telling me to delve more into the subject. I suppose I will keep learning as I go along. So the rejection is not going to kill me. Hey, it may end up being a blessing.

You get the picture now?

By not taking the rejection personally we will be able to diagnose what happened a lot more clearly

And we end up learning more from what transpired.

In addition to 'not taking it personally', psychologists also say that it is important to start with the assumption that *'rejection is part of the game'*. Never enter a situation expecting a perfect result. I don't mean you should be diffident. No, you should be full of confidence. But remember always that rejection can happen. The advice is that you should always be ready to 'expect rejection'. If you are entering with that thought in your mind, when you get the rejection message it is not going to devastate you. It will hurt. It will be painful. But it will not destroy you.

Roman philosopher Seneca said, 'Luck is what happens when preparation meets opportunity.' As a corollary to this, I could add, 'Every rejection holds within it a new opportunity.'

Now let me complete the Madras Central story.. There was a happy ending after all.

Almost an hour after the white open-top luxury sedan had whizzed past the restaurant, we got a call and then a visit from a senior police officer. Apparently, there was a mix up in the instructions given to the police escort. We were told that the Chief Minister was in conversation and had missed signalling the Prime Minister's attache about the stop. So he was deeply apologetic and had suggested that if it was okay, the Prime Minister's cavalcade could stop on its way back from the public meeting.

My grandfather calmly said that he would be honoured and would wait for as long as it took. Sure enough, an hour later, the cavalcade stopped and the garlanding happened.

The rejection turned out to be a false alarm. Maybe you too will have this pleasant experience the next time you face a rejection. Even if you don't, remember, don't take it personally. And be ready to receive it. With a smile.

> **TAKEAWAY:** *Remember to anticipate rejection and keep in mind what is rejected is not 'you' but your idea, your proposal, your CV. Learn to distance yourself from what you presented and dispassionately review the situation.*

The Inner Critic and Some Space Adventures

Don't read success stories, you will only get a message.
Read failure stories and you will get some ideas for success.

—A.P.J. Abdul Kalam

20 July is an important day in the annals of human history. It was on that day in the year 1969 that the American astronaut Neil Armstrong became the first man to set foot on the moon declaring as he stepped on the lunar surface, 'That's one small step for man, one giant leap for mankind.' America's attempt to conquer outer space was not a walk in the park. It had its own shares of failures and rejections.

On 25 May 1961, when President John F. Kennedy made the statement—'I believe that this nation should commit itself to achieving the goal, before this decade is out, of landing a man on the Moon and returning him safely to Earth'—it was a big hairy audacious goal (BHAG as it is called today). It was in a sense America's reaction to the 1957 Sputnik satellite launch by the Soviet Union and the successful human trip into space by the Soviet cosmonaut Yuri Gagarin, in 1961.

American John Glenn became the first American to orbit the earth in 1962 and the NASA Gemini programme created a protocol for sending man into space and practice the rendezvous for docking procedures required for the Apollo missions. But on 27 January 1967, the Apollo programme suffered a major setback with the deaths, in a fire, of three American astronauts. The failure did not set them back by much. In the 1960s, we did not have the constant glare of 24/7 media and social media to hound us in our times of failure.

On 20 July 1969, the scientists at NASA achieved John F. Kennedy's vision, almost six years after his death. The final Apollo 17 mission was in 1972; subsequent missions were cancelled due to budget cuts. The eleven-year space programme cost the US government $25.4 billion (around $160 billion in todays' terms) and twelve men walked or drove a Lunar Rover on the moon.

The American chase to catch up with the Soviets in the space race had its own share of jokes. Here is one: An American astronaut meets a Soviet cosmonaut and proudly shows him the million-dollar pen that the scientists at NASA had developed that could write in a zero-gravity situation. He asks the Soviet, in a condescendingly taunting tone: 'What do you Soviets use to write with when you are in space?' The Soviet smugly replies 'We use a pencil.'

Space missions in every country have had their share of trials and tribulations, failures and rejections, explosions and duds. India is no different.

The late Dr A.P.J. Abdul Kalam, former President of India narrates an interesting tale in his book *You Are Unique*. Professor Satish Dhawan, the then Chairman of ISRO (Indian Space Research Organisation) assigned Dr Kalam the mission of developing India's first satellite launch vehicle (SLV) to put the

Rohini satellite in orbit. The first SLV—3 experimental launch was scheduled to take off on 10 August 1979. A team of fifty, with six specialists, were with Dr Kalam in the control room during the critical launch of the SLV. The team was monitoring all the key parameters with respect to the propulsion system, both the first stage as well as the second stage. Though they noticed a pressure drop in one of the systems they did not call for an abort and so Dr Kalam pushed the button to launch the vehicle. At T-0 the SLV took off wonderfully. The first stage was picture perfect. But things started going badly wrong soon. And the satellite soon tumbled into the Bay of Bengal and was lost.

It is possible Dr Kalam went through a severe sense of self-doubt. Did we not establish a procedure to call for an 'abort'? Did we not have adequate training? Did we not go through multiple scenarios before the real launch? Do we know the technology we were working with? Were we overanxious to succeed?

What was done next by Professor Satish Dhawan is today a part of leadership folklore. In the press conference called to announce the failure, Prof. Dhawan kept Dr Kalam in the background to save him from rejection, criticism and embarrassment. In reality, Dr Kalam was the leader of the mission and should have addressed the press. Instead, Prof. Dhawan himself addressed the press conference and accepted full responsibility for the failure.

To complete the story, when the mission was a resounding success in 1980, Prof. Dhawan kept himself in the sidelines and intentionally asked Dr Kalam to address the press conference to announce the successful launch.

It is not too often that your immediate superior takes on the onus of delivering the bad news, while you may be going through your own remorse, self-doubt and self-criticism.

What Prof. Dhawan created was an environment, and circle of support, for the team that was definitely having its lowest moment.

Scientists like Dr Kalam faced rejection and trying times. And had to face the music, often from the outside and sometimes from the inside as well.

On 8 April 1982, Dr Danny Shechtman, a scientist at Technion Israel Institute of Technology saw something that looked impossible. As he looked at the photos of a rapidly cooling alloy, there were atoms arranged in a pattern that did not repeat itself. They were crystals. Yet they were not. Had he discovered the phenomenon of 'quasi-crystals'? What he noticed should have excited the entire scientific community. But just the opposite happened. His head of research asked him to leave, lest he bring disgrace to the entire university. It broke so many rules that scientists would not accept that he could be right about what he had observed. Dr Linus Pauling, the 'father of molecular biology' and double Nobel Prize winner famously rejected the notion saying, 'There is no such thing as a quasi-crystals, only quasi-scientists.'

Dr Shechtman must have had a severe dose of self-doubt. But he persevered. He found one supporter. Then another. His first paper was rejected. The second was accepted but widely ridiculed by mainstream chemists. But he started gaining increasing belief from mathematicians and physicists outside his narrow domain. And the story had a happy ending. Dr Shechtman was awared the Noble Prize in Chemistry in 2011 for his discovery of, yes, you guessed it right, 'quasi-crystals'. In a *Guardian* (6 June 2013) interview that has a provocative headline 'Linus Pauling said I was talking nonsense', Dr Shechtman speaks emotionally about the rejection horrors he had to face. For a long time, it was Dr Chechtman against the world. He was the subject of ridicule. The leader of the opposition to his findings, Linus Pauling, fought against quasi-periodicity in crystals for years. He was wrong, and after a while, Dr Schechtman started to enjoy every moment of this scientific battle, knowing that Dr Pauling was wrong.

I really enjoyed the last thing he said in the interview. As he started getting support from a wider community, he was no longer in awe of Linus Pauling or his scathing comments. He started to enjoy the duel, knowing that he was right this time.

What happens to you when you get rejected? One of the biggest barriers that you need to handle is inside you. It is your inner critic. When you face rejection, the inner critic starts echoing what the outer world is telling you. Sometimes it starts even before you hear rejection from outside.

Imagine this. You are in an interview at a top-draw firm. You are answering the questions well. Why? Because you had practised the questions and answers well before the interview. But those were practised answers. Your inner voice suddenly murmurs in your ear: Hey, you are not sounding genuine, they are seeing through your answers. You are not really in their league. They are just about tolerating you. You are not able to command their attention. You are a fake.

Thirty minutes into the interview, you are able to take some control and get out of the self-critic mode. You speak about your passion project, the cleaning up of the beach near your home. The interviewer is interested and leans in. You are emboldened and speak passionately about the environment.

As you walk out of the interview, you are feeling a lot better. But your inner critic is still going at you: You blew it there; they were not impressed with you at all; one more good chance blown away; maybe you don't deserve to work in such a good company.

Why is it that we all have an inner critic? Is it there to destroy our self-worth?

Not really. Our inner voice has its good side too. It keeps us on our toes. It makes sure that we don't float in a cloud. But it can also start to have a damaging effect, as an article by Jena E. Pincott in *Psychology Today* (March 2019) says. In the article, Lean Seltzer, a psychologist is quoted as saying, 'You can't ever stop cracking the whip on yourself because you are scared that if you don't, the disapprovals and rejection that seem imminent will become your reality. The stress is unremitting. When you do something well, you won't jump for joy but merely breathe a sigh of relief. You escaped being censured and criticised.'

What purpose does your self-critic serve? Psychologists say that your self-critic is really doing you a good deed. It is preparing you to face rejection from outside. It is giving you the bad news before the outside world gives it to you. This response, this mode of action of self-critic too may be traced to our ancient history and our fear of being rejected by our caregivers.

Let us look at another scenario. You have presented your finding to your senior colleagues. You believe that you have done a lot of good work and dug deep into the data files to find the missing number. But you are hearing voices from inside saying that 'are you really sure?'. Did you run all the statistical tests correctly? Did your young colleague, whom you used as the statistical wizard, really do a good job?

And as these voices start sounding louder and louder, you are on your way to blowing your presentation. And get rejected.

So what is the answer? Your self-critic is trying to do you good. But…?

Prof. Richard Schwartz of Harvard says that some people find success in befriending the self-critic and not treating it as an enemy within. He observes that we have many subpersonalities residing inside us, and our inner critic is just one of them. The inner critic probably has the task of activating our other personalities like 'task master' and 'perfectionist'. Our challenge is to see the inner critic as a protector on our side, looking after our interests, even if it is misguided at times. If our inner critic is making us feel not-good-enough, it is preventing us from a deeper fall.

So what should we do, when our inner critic kicks in. One way is to let it blow steam, thank it for its efforts, but ask for it to step back.

Another way is to create what is called 'self-distancing'—responding to the grievances with a sense of detachment. As if you were another person. So instead of saying, 'Why am I not able to answer this question well', switch it to 'Why is Amit (assuming your name is Amit) not able to answer this question well'. Just moving out of 'I' to 'name', experts say will create a critical distance that you need to regroup your senses.

I think the most important issue that we need to be aware of is that sometimes we are our own worst enemy. Our inner critic works overtime and if we allow it full freedom, it can destroy all the self-confidence we have. We have to develop our own ways of silencing the inner critic and not let it get in the way of us doing our job. It is already a tough life out there. It is difficult to land the better job. It is difficult to get the right assignment, even if you manage to get into the better company. And if you allow your inner self critic to run wild, you will end up getting pounded to pulp. We need the inner critic. It is our conscience keeper. But we need to be aware that it can at times become overbearing.

Dr Kalam was lucky that when his inner critic was probably working overtime after the SLV-3 disaster, he had the support of Prof. Dhawan, who shielded him from the prying eyes of the media. A lethal cocktail was not allowed to blow up—the inner critic getting further fuel from external criticism.

To those of us who run teams, there is a big lesson from what we can learn from Prof. Dhawan. When our team has failed to deliver, what is our responsibility? The team knows that they have let you down. Their inner critic is possibly working extra hard to tell them that they are worthless. Can we at that moment awaken the Prof. Dhawan inside us? How can we temper our own feedback? Is it possible to take the blame when your team fails but be generous to them when they succeed? Often we end up doing just the opposite. Blame the team when they fail. And take the credit when they succeed.

We need to switch the narrative. Be more selfish during failure and rejection (I want to take this on myself) and be more generous during success (you guys deserve all the credit).

If we can do this, then our teams will be able to quieten their own inner critic and perform at even higher levels.

Not all of us will be lucky to get a superior like Prof. Dhawan. We may have to face the music after the rocket falls into the bay. At that time, we cannot allow our inner critic to join forces with the external voices baying for our blood. We need to get the inner critic to shut up so that we can figure out a way of regrouping our resources.

> **TAKEAWAY:** *Before you face rejection from outside, be ready to face the inner critic. Never let your inner critic demotivate you. Listen to the inner critic, but be aware that your inner critic is always more harsh than the outside world. This is because it is giving you the rejection vaccine.*

part two

PROCESSING AND RECOVERING FROM REJECTION

Springs are resilient structures designed to undergo large deflections within their elastic range.

—Standard Handbook of Machine Design

Hardening is the second step in the creation of a spring. The steel which has been coiled has a lot of internal stress, to relieve this stress the spring is tempered by heat treating it.

Making It to the A Team

*Never give up! Failure and rejection are only
the first step to succeeding.*

—Jim Valvano, American Basketball Player,
Coach, Broadcaster

He was a short, thin kid in school. But he could outrun all his classmates. And when armed with a hockey stick, he could outmanoeuvre anyone. The ball seemed glued to his hockey stick. Viren Rasquinha is your typical Bandra kid, who enjoyed his game of hockey. He was seen as a prodigy and a sure shot player for the state and the country too. But he was rejected by the Mumbai hockey team selection committee four times. Dealing with rejection became a habit. And interestingly, he got selected to play for the India Juniors Hockey team before he got a nod from Mumbai. Cutting them some slack, he says with no rancour, 'The Mumbai team was among the best those days.'

Viren was indeed fortunate to have his parents solidly behind him. Even the very liberal Bandra community did not think highly of his pursuit in sports. And when he did not get selected by the Mumbai team it was a big blow. When you get rejected you can take it as a body blow, or you can come back stronger. Viren says philosophically, 'The sun will rise tomorrow.' His intense belief in his skills did not let him down. He ended up playing for India and captaining the Indian hockey team at the Olympics.

Viren says that if you don't face rejection in sports, you can't improve. After completing an MBA from the Indian School of Business (ISB), Hyderabad, Viren is now the CEO of Olympic Gold Quest (OGQ), a not-for-profit organisation that is focused on getting India more medals at the Olympics. He and his team spend time mentoring and helping young athletes as they face rejection and heartbreak, objections and hurdles.

Viren is full of stories of how India's sportspersons face the anguish of rejection. There is no single formula to handle rejection in sports. And each successful sportsperson has his or her own formula.

Gagan Narang when he missed winning a medal in the 10m Air Rifle contest at Beijing Olympics (2008) by a narrow margin, was so dejected, that he did not shoot for a full year. But then he came back, committed himself fully and then went on to win a bronze at the London Olympics (2012).

P.V. Sindhu, the badminton sensation, won many medals including gold as a youngster, but when she entered the Super Series at the age of seventeen she lost in the first round; in the next tournament it was a second-round defeat. Match after match, she tasted defeat. But surrounded by a good team, a coach (Pullela Gopichand) who believed in her, OGQ and her parents, she got back her mojo and went on to win championship after championship.

Srikanth Kidambi too had to struggle with this transition and managed to hit his stride only when he turned twenty-one.

Viren points out that the biggest challenge for sportspersons is to transition successfully from being a champion junior to a champion senior. And to do that they have to develop an ability to process failure and rejection. They cannot start doubting their game. They need to remember something fundamental.

Form is temporary. But class is permanent.

Remembering his days at ISB, Viren says that the whizkids from IIT who were in his class at ISB suddenly found themselves at a loss in the case discussions. Just as sports persons find it difficult to adapt from a junior level to a senior level game, these tech-nerds suddenly realised that they needed a different set of skills to handle a complex business case discussion. Just having great computer programming skills would not take one very far.

When a sports person reaches the top, is the job done? Do you then just coast along? Not at all, because failure and rejection are waiting around a corner.

Prakash Padukone at the age of twenty-seven was at the top of his game. But he decided that he was not good enough and moved to Denmark where he could get better coaches and practice partners. Moving to a strange country, in the 1980s, with his wife was a very bold move. Obviously, this was triggered by his intense desire to get even better than what he was. And mind you, he was among the best.

Or take Geet Sethi, after winning his third world snooker championship decided to learn everything from scratch, once again. He did start losing as he was perfecting a new game. But he was obsessed with getting to a better place. Finally, he hit his stride and went on to win six more world titles.

Interestingly, Geet Sethi and Prakash Padukone are two of the founders of OGQ.

On the other side of the world, Tiger Woods too has had his share of rejections, health issues and personal challenges. But he has been a comeback champion for more than two decades. He rises to the top of his game, just when everyone has written him off.

What does it take to get back into the groove after facing rejection?

Geet Sethi writes in his book *Success vs Joy* (co-authored with Sunil Agarwal), 'I met Rahul Dravid a few weeks after he was first dropped from the Indian cricket team. I was training at the Kanteerva Stadium in Bangalore as part of our preparation for the Asian Games to be held in Bangkok in 1998. I saw him pushing himself to the limit. He was working on his physical fitness. His trainer Bidu was throwing a heavy sand-filled ball the size of a football at him. Rahul himself was lying on his stomach and was catching the ball above his head. This is a difficult enough exercise to do with a cricket ball, but with a heavy ball it becomes almost impossible… He later said that he felt the need to work on his upper body fitness. Every morning he was there, earlier than all the other state-level athletes who trained in the stadium. He had no regrets about being dropped from the team at that time.'

Rahul Dravid's reaction to rejection was very different from that of Gagan Narang. So there is no one formula to process rejection. Some athletes just step back to get their co-ordinates together. Some of them brush off the rejection in a jiffy and are back to the training field.

Paddy Upton is a much-capped South African cricket player who has transitioned into being an executive coach and academic. He was hired by the Indian team management to be the mental conditioning coach during the run up to the 2011 ICC Cricket World Cup. He partnered with yet another successful South African cricketer, Gary Kristen to help the Indian team lift the World Cup in 2011. In his book, *The Barefoot Coach*, Paddy Upton puts down what he believes are the 'Seven Habits of Highly Effective Losers':

1. Gaining perspective—View the loss or rejection in the context of its limits. Don't make it affect your larger life.
2. Expect and accept failure as a part of life and learning.
3. Know that this too shall pass (The sun will rise tomorrow, as Viren said).
4. Control the controllables—Take action to control what you can and accept what you cannot control.
5. Review to learn—Express emotions, don't bottle them up and take time to see what worked and what did not work.
6. Plan to improve—Focus on the next opportunity (like Rahul Dravid in the Kanteerava Stadium) and doing better there.
7. Grow character—Win or lose, be a good person, your results do not determine who you are as a person.

Seven Habits of Highy Effective Losers—Paddy Upton

1. Gain perspective
2. Expect and accept failure
3. Know that this too shall pass
4. Control the controllables
5. Review to learn
6. Plan to improve
7. Grow character

Michael Jordan, the basketball legend has said, 'I've missed more than 9000 shots in my career. I've lost almost 300 games. Twenty-six times I have been trusted to take the game winning shot and missed. I've failed over and over and over again in my life. And that is why I succeed.'

I found that quote amazing in many ways. It is an admission of one's own blemishes and faults. Yet acknowledging that those are an integral part of who you see yourself to be.

Nick Bollettieri is possibly the most famous tennis coach ever. He pioneered the concept of a tennis boarding cchool. The numerous tennis champions he has coached include Andre Agassi, Jim Courier, Monica Seles, Venus and Serena Williams, Martina Hingis and Maria Sharapova. When asked what makes for a tennis champions or athletes for life, he identified the following:

1. Believe in yourself, because if you don't believe in yourself, no one else will.
2. You must surround yourself with the support system that has the same passion and belief (like you) that will

tell you things that you don't want to hear and without a support team you can't do it.

3. No matter how good you are, everybody must consider adjustments and sometimes making major changes.

4. Passion, not to be one of the best, but to be the very best.

In your line of work, you will face rejection and failure. How are you going to process these setbacks? Will you blame yourself and get into a long downward spiral? Or will you see that as a part of your journey and get back to practising your game sincerely once again. Will you find people to help you improve your game? And will you be ready to accept harsh criticism so that you can play better?

When I was at IIT we had a genius at chess, my old friend Balu. He was popularly known as Chess Balu. But in 1975, India was not a force in chess. And we used to wonder when India would produce its first Grandmaster. We tried goading Balu but to no avail. So it was in 1988 that India got its first Grandmaster in Vishwanathan 'Vishy' Anand. He went on to become the World Champion and single-handedly helped inspire numerous Indian kids to take up chess and excel. As of July 2019, there were as many as sixty-four Grandmasters in India. Vishy says that when you win, '… you're certainly happy, but there is also relief.' But when you lose: '… defeats are when you want to separate yourself from the person who played. Forget the tournament. Get home yesterday and burn the whole memory down.'

To me the lessons I learnt speaking with sportspersons and reading about them say one thing very clearly. Even the topmost athletes face rejection and failure. And what sets the champions apart is their ability to process and handle the rejection. As Viren pointed out, it helps to have a team to work with you on your journey. In fact, individual athletes, unlike in a team sport, have a steeper upward climb. And it is here that they are today being helped by organisations like OGQ.

Reaching out when you face rejection

Whom will you reach out to when you face rejection? Do you have a confidante (maybe, several confidantes) whom you can go to for help? And how sure are you that they have your success at heart? Are they ready to tell you the bitter truth, and not sugarcoat it for your benefit?

If you are unsure about your answers to the above questions, it is time you sat back and figured out what you need to do. For example, your parents may be great for rubbing a salve on your wounds. But will they be able to help you rediscover your inner core? Yes, they play a very vital role to help you keep your self-confidence. But sometimes they may even mislead you: 'Don't worry. That was not a good company for you to work in. You will get something *muuuuchhh* better, beta'. This does not help except as a cold compress on a throbbing elbow.

You need to figure out who is going to be in your inner team to help you get to the next level. It may be a college friend, it may be a former boss, it may be a well-meaning professor of yours. But do the soul searching now, when you don't need them. It will be foolhardy to assemble a team when you are down in the dumps. You will end up picking the wrong people to be in your team, if you are doing it in a hurry.

Once you have your core group, be ready to help them, just as you are wanting their help. So offer your time. Offer your unbiased feedback. Give negative feedback and tell them you too welcome negative feedback. I don't for a minute mean that you should become rude or insulting.

Become 'empathetically assertive' as Adrienne Green and John Humphrey point out in their book, *Coaching for Resilience*. Make your point assertively but be empathetic and show emotion in a positive way. Be able to take control of your own life and live according to your own wishes, needs and values, while always taking into account the wishes, needs and values of others.

Tim Hartford's basic lesson (in his book *Adapt*) is you have to *design your life to make effective use of failures.* You have to design systems of trial and error, or to use a natural word, evolution. Most successful enterprises are built through a process of groping and adaptation, not planning. Russian thinker Peter Palchinsky understood the basic structure of smart change. First, seek out new ideas and new things. Next, try new things on a scale small enough so that their failure is survivable. Then find a feedback mechanism so you can tell which new thing is failing and which is succeeding. That's the model—variation, survivability, selection.

Whether you are getting ready to play your biggest game, or preparing to present your dream project to your bosses or have to appear for the most important interview of your life, remember the lessons that these sportspersons have shared with us.

Jeffrey A. Sonnenfeld and Andrew J. Ward in their article 'Firing Back: How Great Leaders Rebound After Career

Disasters' in the *Harvard Business Review* (January 2007) have these end comments that are very appropriate for us to remember: 'No one can truly define success and failure for us—only we can define that for ourselves. No one can take away our dignity unless we surrender it. No one can take away our hope and pride unless we relinquish them. No one can steal our creativity, imagination and skills unless we stop thinking. No one can stop us from rebounding unless we give up.'

You too should be ready to process rejection and get back on your feet, to prepare for the next test. The next match. The rejection cannot be allowed to define who you are. That is something that is entirely in your hands. And remember springing back is in your hands. Always.

> **TAKEAWAY:** *Like successful sportsmen and sportswomen, don't let a rejection kill your spirit. Learn to process rejection better. Build ways of recovering from rejection and practice even harder. You will finally make it to the A Team.*

The Magic of Reframing

The way to change the game is to change the frame.

—William Ury, author of the
negotiation classic *Getting to Yes*

When I moved from Chennai to Mumbai in 1994, I was told that I would be working on two of the most exciting brands that the ad agency Ulka handled in Mumbai. One was ITC's Sundrop cooking oil, a brand I was familiar with as I used to handle a small part of the Hyderabad-based ITC Agro-Tech's local brand communication needs as a part of my South Zone duties. But, the other brand, Santoor, I thought would be a great new account for me to learn about and work on.

To those who may not be aware, Santoor from Wipro was a client the agency had bagged after a rather long pitch process in 1988-89. The brand had been launched in the early/mid 1980s and had performed reasonably well in its launch phase. It had then slowed down and Wipro after much deliberation decided to move the account to Ulka. The brand's advertising was drastically revamped from ingredient-oriented advertising—'this soap contains sandal and turmeric'—to benefit-oriented advertising—'the sandal and turmeric in this soap will keep you looking young'. The creative device used in the advertising was what was called 'mistaken identity'; a mother of a young girl gets mistaken for someone much younger—a college student, or a teenager. The campaign had been a resounding success and sales had gone through the roof, from 1989 to 1992.

My job, I was told, was to carry forward the legacy. I did not know, then, that I was going to be facing or untangling a big 'rejection problem'.

The reality was that the brand had started slowing down in late 1992 and in 1993, its sales had actually declined. The agency was asked to recreate the magic that had saved the brand in 1989. The agency's answer was a film that we called 'Jazz'. It featured a woman in a dance or what could be called an aerobics class with a group of young girls who gets mistaken for a college girl, till her daughter appears in the scene calling her 'mummy'. The agency or at least the MD of the agency was convinced that Santoor had got trapped in a 'wedding' and 'tradition' trap and needed to move into a more modern setting, without sacrificing the sandal-turmeric story and the 'younger-looking skin' promise. The film that the agency hard sold to the client was tested with consumers through the tried and tested focus group method. But it did not test well. The client wanted the agency to explore alternative routes. Why stick with the younger-looking skin premise? Why continue with the hackneyed 'mummy' call? Why not play up the ingredients in a different way? Why couldn't the agency think of other ways of telling the story?

Truth be told, even in the agency camp there were some doubting Thomases. We did have a few who were not sure about the longevity of the younger-looking skin, mummy story. The agency had created alternative creative concepts, but fortunately or unfortunately, they too did not test well with consumers.

There was an impasse and this went on for more than six months. The story goes that in one of the meetings the then-CEO of the Wipro Consumer Care division, P.S. Pai, handed over a copy of the book *Positioning* by Al Ries and Jack Trout to the MD of the agency saying, 'This may inspire you to think of something better.'

When I came on board, I did not know all these gory details. Wipro had meanwhile been told that the agency was planning to change the team on the account and would figure out a solution.

As I took charge of the account in May 1994, I realised that the younger-looking skin and 'mummy' promise still had legs. Great brand campaigns can run literally unchanged for decades and this campaign was hardly five years old. But there was an impasse. The divide between the agency and the client seemed unsurmountable. I admired the patience displayed by Wipro even as their brand sales was suffering for want of advertising. Today, the agency would likely have got the boot and a new agency empanelled in a few weeks. But those were different days, I suppose.

I was told that my mandate was to preserve the core brand story. So, I had to go back and sell 'Jazz'. I realised that even the name of the ad was wrong and sent the wrong signals. Agencies love to give titles to ads. Vicariously, the creative director thinks he is making a feature film, I suppose. I was told, 'Our target consumers in Karnataka and Kerala don't know jazz. You guys from South Mumbai should go out and meet the consumers who are buying Santoor!' If the same film had been titled 'Aerobics Class' or 'Dance Class', it may have made sense. But back to the hot potato that was on my lap.

The agency leadership wanted me to save the idea. The client meanwhile was not keen on putting money behind something that in his opinion, their consumers would not even understand.

Let us stop for a minute and see how this rejection problem can be handled

Did I have the option of walking out? No, it was a very important piece of business for the agency.

Did I have the option of dropping the idea and moving with another? The boss man in the agency would have skinned me alive, but I also knew that the alternatives tested did not do too well.

So I had to dig deeper to understand and process the rejection better. As I got talking with the client team I realised that their problem was not with the younger-looking skin or 'mummy' but with the format we had got stuck in. Over four years the agency had stayed with several renditions of marriage and wedding.

I saw an opening at the end of several discussions. I had to 'reframe' the narrative.

As we got speaking in the office I realised that the way out of the rejection was to change the frame of evaluation. What if we took the same concept, but created two stories. We had one which was 'Jazz' or 'Aerobics'. What if there was one more which is not so 'South Bombay'. On a flight back from Cochin to Mumbai I explained the idea to the big boss: the story is set in a music store; our heroine picks up a flute and starts playing; two young girls admire her flute playing and ask her if she was in their college; a little girl runs in shouting 'mummy'.

We now had two stories to present to the client. The rejection had been reframed. And we thought we had a way out of the challenge. The agency still felt that 'Aerobics' would work, but was okay with 'Music Store' story too.

The client team understood that there was a way out of the challenge, and they green lighted the production of both films. The idea was to run 'Music Store' in South India and 'Aerobics' in North India. The now legendary ad film maker Prahlad Kakkar was tasked with making 'Aerobics' and the inhouse director Subodh Poddar was asked to make the 'Music Store' film.

In three months, from rejection and no film on air, we had moved to a problem of plenty. When the two films were finally ready, both at the agency and the client had a tough time picking their favourite. What later transpired was even more interesting. The client decided to put both the fully produced films into consumer research in Karnataka and Andhra Pradesh. Consumers loved the 'Aerobics' while mildly liking the 'Music Store' film.

In the end, the 'Music Store' film hardly ran for a month, soon to be replaced by 'Aerobics' in even the more traditional markets of Kerala and Karnataka. Sales of the brand started to pick up again.

The tactical move to create two films worked and the brand till date has stayed with the younger-looking skin, 'mummy' format.

Have you faced a rejection that could have been saved by a 'reframing'?

What can you learn from this story? Can you relate what transpired to something that you may have gone through?

Vipin Suri was the visionary hotelier who set up ITC Sea Rock Hotel in Mumbai and later the ITC Mughal Sheraton. He later became a trainer and a coach. During my days at UDI Yellow Pages we had asked Vipin to do a series of sales training programmes for us. Vipin once told me this classic training he conducted for stewards at all the restaurants he ran. You never asked a customer whether they would have dessert. You also don't ask them what they would have for dessert. Instead you asked them, 'What will it be for dessert, madam, vanilla or strawberry?' By asking this question you have eliminated the possibility of 'no dessert'. If you asked the question 'Will you have dessert?', you might get a 'no'. But with the question, 'We have some terrific gulab jamuns and real authentic kulfi. So what will it be for dessert, madam?', you effectively guide the customer to a place where it is easy for them to take a decision. They may ask, 'What else do you have', which is a good place to go. In fact, anything is better than 'No dessert, please' if you are running a restaurant.

In a similar vein, the idea of creating two options can change the narrative around 'rejection'.

The next time your proposal gets rejected, remember you could save it by reframing the proposal. Moving from 'Jazz' to 'Aerobics' could put you back in the reckoning. But better still is to think of an alternative that can help you get a chance to pitch the original idea once again.

One important caution though. You need to get behind the rejection and process it differently, before you try your hand at reframing. The strategy of reframing can work only if the rejection left some wiggle room for you to re-argue the case. One option is to try and re-present the case with new arguments in favour of the case.

Let me illustrate this again. You have been given an important assignment on cost reduction. You have examined all the cost numbers, spoken with the teams involved and identified technology partners. You have spent not less than thirty working days on the project. You feel that you have a watertight case to implement a plan that can save the company as much as 3 per cent of the administrative costs incurred every year. Your presentation to the Management Board goes well but in the end your proposal is rejected. You are told that your manpower cut is not in line with the company's tradition and you are betting too heavily on some unproven technology. You try arguing your case, but after a point you realise that you have lost the battle. The Board asks you to rework your plan and also think afresh.

Was It a rejection? Or will you attempt a reframing?

One option is to drop your original plan and start working afresh on a new plan. The other is to do a bit of tinkering of the first plan and go back.

The best solution may be an intermediate option. You should work on a new plan, which makes a set of new assumptions, about manpower, technology and so on. When you present your new plan, you should also present your earlier version, so that it is clear that you believe that the Board should look at both before deciding.

In my experience, the Board may have questioned you because they were testing your conviction on what you have proposed. As you unfold your new plan, they will see that you are able to think afresh and come with new solutions, albeit not as good as the first one. Often we make the mistake of abandoning the first option. If you were to present the old option once again, the Board gets to compare the two to take a more informed decision. Just as it happened at Wipro.

In the article 'How to Bounce Back from Adversity' Joshua Margolis and Paul Strolz say '… to strengthen their resilience managers need to shift from reflexive, cause-oriented thinking to active response-oriented thinking.'

There are four components to these modes of thinking: **control**, **impact**, **breadth** and **duration**.

Take Control: Instead of lamenting about whether the adverse event was inevitable or could you have prevented it, you could think of asking the question, 'What features of the situation can I (even potentially) improve?'

Negotiation training often hinges on getting you to learn to reframe a rejection. The most often asked question in negotiation is this one:

'How will you split a pizza between two warring kids?'

The first answer is to get one kid to cut the pizza with the condition that his brother will have the first choice. See how that works. If the cutter makes disproportionate sizes, his brother can pick the bigger piece, since he gets the first choice.

In the book *Getting to Yes*, the gurus of negotiation research and training, Robert Fisher and William Ury, say that there could be a better method. What if you spent time finding out what the kids like in the pizza? Do they like the same parts? Or is there a difference in what they really enjoy? You may find that the younger kid likes the outer rind part of the pizza while the elder kid likes the centre section. So you now have a better solution. Instead of cutting the pizza the usual way, you could then make two concentric circles. The outer one for the younger fellow and the inner circle for the elder kid.

Sundar Pichai became the CEO of Alphabet, the owner of Google, in December 2019. His rise in the company which he joined in 2004 has been nothing short of astronomical. But during his journey in Google he did face many rejections. But he didn't take no for an answer. The first time he pitched the idea for Chrome, it was shot down for being 'too expensive'. He then compiled data and built a case, after which the project was green-lit. Chrome soon became the most popular search engine across platforms and devices. It grew into more than just a browser.

The next time you face a rejection think of applying the reframing concept to get out of the problem. What you see as a rejection in the first pass may not in fact be a hard rejection. Can you get deeper into the process of how the proposal got rejected? Are there some areas that can be probed for a better understanding? And if you find out more, what can you do to get the rejection decision reversed. Remember someone who has rejected something you have presented is not going to approve it in a jiffy. You need to understand human psychology. By reversing his decision he is going to admit he was wrong.

That is not going to happen. However, if you can help the decision-maker relook at his decision by providing more data, more options and more proof, you may actually be able to get the decision reversed.

You may well end up selling your original idea. And will be able to spring out of a tricky situation to a much better place.

> **TAKEAWAY:** *When rejected, don't despair but learn to process the rejection better. Look back and see what was rejected. Is there a way of reframing the offer to improve its appeal to the target customer? Explore new frames of references before you give up on a good idea.*

Multiple Shades of Rejection

It is necessary to put yourself out for rejection,
and accept that you will be rejected.

—Robert Genn, Canadian Artist

Have you ever been 'mildly rejected'—where you got a feeling that you had been rejected, but were not too sure if you had been rejected or not?

Those of us who are very thin-skinned may interpret certain situations as a rejection. Those with thicker skin may interpret it not as rejection at all, but as a mild put-off. Some of us may even see it as a 'buying signal' and may rationalise to say that if they had wanted to reject it, they would have said so. 'Buying Signal' is a term used in professional sales training. Salespeople are taught how to spot the buying signal. Questions such as what is the price, when can you deliver and so on are said to be buying signals.

Can a mild rejection be turned into a career-defining move? Here is something that happened. I have of course changed the names to avoid causing any untoward embarrassment to the person concerned.

My assistant buzzed me to say that Basu Biswas was on the line. I took the call immediately. You could not make Basu wait. That was a lesson I had learnt early in my life at FCB Ulka. Basu was a colleague for many years in Ulka before he set up an ad agency of his own with yet another colleague, Ashok Agarwal. We continued to be good friends, trading gossip about the industry and more. Basu was of a highly helpful nature and often his call would be to ensure a friend's son or daughter got a summer internship or an entry-level job at the agency. This time, I was not really ready for such a request. The year was looking difficult and we were not hiring any new talent, even at entry levels. And our yearly recruitment of management trainees was done.

Basu had an interesting request. He said that one of his best servicing executives' husband, who was currently working in a small agency was keen on joining a large agency. I tried fobbing off Basu saying that we were not hiring at all. But Basu insisted that I should meet this guy for what it was worth. I need not offer him a job, but meet him, I must. I reluctantly agreed. I told Basu to ask this guy, whom we will call DK, to call me on my direct line at the office.

Within a few hours I had got a call from DK. I explained to DK that I would be happy to meet him but was badly tied up for the next four weeks. If he was still interested, he could reach me four weeks later.

Almost to the exact date, DK called me, four weeks later. I was not sure what to do with DK. I did not have a role in my mind for him. So I decided to give him the royal run-around. I asked him to call me three weeks late, hoping that he would land a job somewhere else and I would be off the hook.

Remember where we started; mild rejection.

Again, three weeks later DK was on the line. Reminding me that I had asked him to call me three weeks later.

This charade continued for another four to six weeks. DK was always prompt in making the calls. I could set my watch or my calendar by his calls. It was exactly two weeks or three weeks as I kept indicating. A random date if you get the drift.

Finally, I agreed to meet DK.

As luck would have it, just a few days, before I was to meet DK we suddenly had an opening in the Direct Marketing division of the agency. It was a client servicing job, but was in the Direct arm which involved a fair bit of co-ordination with activation and other peripheral service providers. A classical mainline client servicing person may not find it interesting was my view and hence I was not sure about DK.

On the given day, DK landed up at my office. I liked his sincerity and honesty. He was an MBA from one of the lesser-known B-Schools of Mumbai but was burning with enthusiasm. He was keen on working in a large established ad agency on a large advertising account, to build his career. From what I could make out, he was passionate about advertising and marketing. I spent an hour with him and then asked him if he was willing to work in the Direct Marketing division. I warned him that though he would work on a big account, the job was going to be a lot more mundane that he would imagine. In fact, the job would not be very different from what he was doing in the small agency where he was currently working. DK jumped at the opportunity, though he knew very little about how direct marketing worked. When asked, he replied, 'Sir, I am sure you and your colleagues will be able teach me what Direct Marketing is all about. Just working in this agency will be great learning for me.' I got him to meet the head of the Direct Division and the deal was sealed a few days later.

Thinking back, what worked in DK's favour? Was it his never-say-die attitude? Or was it his very polite but consistent follow-ups? Never did he call before or after the set deadline. And he was utterly professional in his call. Never pleading, never cloying, never aggressive. Not once did he say, 'Sir, meet me at least once, Sir. Basu Sir promised me that you would meet me.' No, he kept it absolutely professional. He was confident about his talent. And wanted to be hired at the right time for the right reasons. I respected him for that. Truly. Now to the story of what happened after he joined the agency.

DK was assigned to work on the Tata Motors account and the agency's Direct Marketing division was working on the Tata Indica CRM programme. The agency team had created a robust way of collecting customer details, often from the service cards at dealer points. The addresses were cross-verified and stored in the agency computer system. The Indica Club, as it was known, was one of the earliest CRM programmes run by a car company in India. One of the interesting things we did was to welcome each new Indica owner with a small welcome kit. In the brainstorming meeting on what to send to new car owners, someone suggested that we could send one of those 'sun shades' that go on the windshied of a car, to protect it from overheating when it was parked in open sunlight.

It was DK who suggested that we should get some interesting design printed on the sun shade. The idea was to get someone like the famous cartoonist Mario Miranda to do a special cartoon of Tata Indica with Mumbai skyline and some of Mario's favourite characters. DK offered to locate Mario Miranda and pitch the idea to him. We had limited budgets for the cartoon and we wished DK all the best in his attempt.

DK was a resourceful fellow. He managed to locate Mario Miranda in a few days. The famous cartoonist had moved to Goa by then. He spoke with Mario and discovered that Mario (or his wife) owned a Tata Indica. In fact, they had received the Indica Club newsletters in their Goa home. DK was thrilled and managed to negotiate a modest fee to be paid to Mario for the cartoon. Let me say that the Indica sun shade was a big hit. The original cartoon went on to adorn the Bombay House cabin of Rajiv Dube, the director of the passenger car division of Tata Motors, for many years.

DK left FCB Ulka a few years later to join a large bank and has since built an outstanding career in the financial services sector. He is today one of the most respected marketing professionals in the BFSI (Banking Financial Services Insurance) sector and he continues to be active in creating innovative marketing programmes for his company.

I wonder if I would have been able to stomach the 'mild rejection' that I subjected DK to. But because DK was able to take the 'mild rejection' with a smile he got to a much better place.

Landing a job in a dream company is often a cat-and-mouse game, a slow and steady process. To this day, I feel a bit guilty for having made DK wait. But my good friend R. Sridhar had this tale to narrate that kind of assuaged my guilt feelings.

R. Sridhar is today a much-in-demand innovation coach, TEDx speaker, author. He had a stellar career in one of India's top ad agencies, Ogilvy & Mather before he stepped out to start on his coaching journey. He did not land a job in Ogilvy that easily. He had started his career in a small but highly respected agency but knew he had to get into a bigger company where the learning opportunities would be more. He managed to wangle an interview with Mr Mani S.R. Iyer of Ogilvy & Mather. The interview went well. Mr Iyer got him to meet the Bombay branch head who too liked Sridhar. Then Mr Iyer bowled a bouncer. He told Sridhar that at the present moment they did not have an opening. So Sridhar should call back a month later. Sridhar could have interpreted it as a rejection, but he saw it as an opportunity to speak with Mr Iyer once again. So a month later, Sridhar called Mr Iyer but was told to call a month later. This went on for five months. Finally, Mr Iyer asked Sridhar to come and meet him, only to offer him a position in the Chennai (then Madras) office. Sridhar grabbed it with both hands. He went to Chennai, and then to Bangalore. He worked on the trailblazing Titan campaign, created India's first Direct Marketing Agency and went on to join the board of Ogilvy & Mather. Remember this journey started with a mild rejection: 'Call me next month'.

Nitesh Tiwari is a well-known name in the Bollywood industry. He is a national award winner for his children's film, *Chillar Party* and is also the director of one of the biggest Bollywood grossers of this decade, *Dangal*. Not many of you may know that he is also a BTech from IIT Mumbai. Fewer people may know that he started his career as a Hindi copy trainee at FCB Ulka Advertising.

Here is the story.

I was handed over an envelope by my assistant saying that someone had come and dropped it off at the reception. It was a letter from a young man called Nitesh Tiwari. In the letter he explained that he had just completed his BTech from IIT Mumbai and though he had a job with an IT services major, he was wanting to work in advertising, especially in Hindi copywriting. He had enclosed several sheets of paper, specimens of his writing in Hindi that included a longish poem. I managed to read the poem which was rather humourous and had an intriguing title: 'Me and My Neighbour's Dog'. Since my Hindi is patchy at best, I decided to show the entire set of papers to my colleague Shashi Sinha, who in a minute said, 'We should hire this guy.' The sentiment was echoed by Subhas Tendle, one of our veteran creative directors the next day.

I was given the job of calling Nitesh and finding out if he was really keen on the job. Starting salaries for copy trainees in ad agencies were not in the same league as what a BTech would command in a TCS or Wipro. In fact, a copy trainee starts at the lowest level of the agency pay grade. I called Nitesh and had a long conversation. I thought I had tried to present the 'reality' to him with all the downsides. Shashi too met him and explained the positives and the negatives. I later discovered that Nitesh got Shashi to call his father in Bhopal to explain that advertising is a respectable profession for a BTech. (Shashi should know, as he too was from one of the IITs.)

Some days after Nitesh had joined us, I asked him how he got to send his CV and poems to us. Why our agency? He replied that he had sent the same envelope to ten agencies.

Only FCB Ulka had called him for an interview. If I had asked him what would he have done if we had not called, he would have probably replied that he would have sent out the same letter again, or a longer letter to another ten agencies.

A person like Nitish was not going to stop at 'no' for an answer. He would have pursued his dream till he got where he wanted to be. No rejection was going to stop him.

To complete the story, Nitesh was one of the most prolific writers in the agency. After four years at FCB Ulka, he moved to Lowe Lintas and then to Leo Burnett, from where he moved to pursue his passion in film-making. His children's film *Chillar Party* won the national film award of best children's film in 2011. His supernatural political drama film *Bhoothnath Returns* released in 2014 was a box office hit. And in 2016, he wrote and directed *Dangal* which ended up becoming one of the highest-grossing Hindi films ever. And he started his journey into the creative world of films by mailing envelopes to total strangers, hoping that one of them would open the envelope, read the contents and call him.

Miracles do happen, if you are ready to ignore mild rejection signals and keep at it till Lady Luck smiles

What do these three stories teach us about rejection? For one, there are various types of rejections. There is the hard one, and DK could have got a signal that there was no point in trying to meet this guy (me) who was playing hard to get and there was no way he was going to get a job there. The signal he got was a mild one and he decided to interpret it as a very mild rejection. He kept his spirits up and kept trying as per the dates given to him. He was never once impolite or rude. Never did he try to hustle his way into a meeting.

Let us play this scenario out in sales. You are keen on meeting the purchase manager of the company. Or it could be the admin head. Or the HR head. You never ever manage to get through to the right person in the first attempt. It is often the secretary who holds the keys to the kingdom. Sometimes she may on her own volition say, 'Boss is very busy'. Sometimes she may say, 'Let me check,' and then say, 'Sorry, he is busy right now.' Often this means, 'He is not interested in meeting you or talking with you.'

One lesson after many years of playing a business development role is that it is critical for you to befriend the secretary. Knowing her name, addressing her with respect, enlisting her support are possibly the oldest tricks of the cold-calling trade.

When being fobbed off we can give up and put down the phone. But do a bit of visualising. What would DK have done. Here are a few options.

DK would have sweet-talked the secretary to find out when the boss would be relatively free so that he could call. Or he would have spoken with her as if she was the decision-maker. This often ends up making the secretary sympathetic and sometimes even offer her inputs on how to wangle a meeting from her elusive boss. The other simple method is to say, 'I will call again next week. I hope he is in town.'

Those of us who have been in an active business development role know that we face mild rejections all the time. We often give up going the full distance. I have been at the receiving end too many times to count. And I have at times managed to get through to the key decision-maker after not one or two, but as many as twenty attempts. The boss sometimes even apologises, 'Sorry, I know you have been trying to meet me, but I have been very busy.' You acknowledge that with a smile and get down to business. Both parties know that you have been trying hard and have finally been rewarded.

Sometimes you need to create new windows to meet a much-in-demand person

This friend of mine was trying to do a fundraiser for his NGO. He had established contact with a senior director in a large company that had similar CSR goals as the NGO. But the company was based in Delhi and my friend was in Bangalore. The director discouraged my friend from making a trip to Delhi, but showed keenness in meeting him. But the director's trips to Bangalore were always packed. How to squeeze in the time? Our friend managed to find a window. He requested the director to let him travel in his car from the airport to the Bangalore office. The sixty minutes worked like a charm. The company became a long-term sponsor of the NGO. A mild rejection turned into a positive endorsement.

In scouting for new business in advertising or any other industry, it is almost mandatory that you should meet the potential customer, well before they decide to float a 'Request For Proposal' (RFP). When asked, 'Why are you inviting this agency, they are not in the same league as your other three short-listed agencies', clients often reply, 'They have been chasing us for months and we appreciate the hunger they have shown for our business. They may not be as big or as reputable as the others who are invited, but they seem to be absolutely keen to work with us. Do you know they have been calling us every week, for the last six months?'

I have heard from friends in the IT Services sector that you can never win a pitch if the RFP came to you in your inbox, from a customer you did not know or meet.

This is probably true in every industry. What is the way out of this? How can you ensure that you meet all potential clients before they put out an RFP?

And when you get invited to present, how do you make sure you manage the rejections?

Xerox had possibly the best sales training programme in the world. Their patented 'Personal Selling Skills' (PSS) workshop usually lasted six days and there was a time when everyone in sales, in all the Xerox units across the world, went through this programme every year. Irrespective of their level, experience or title. In PSS there is a whole module on handling rejection and looking for 'buying signals'. For example if the customer says, 'But your machine is so expensive, we cannot ever afford to buy one', it can be interpreted as a rejection. Xerox training gets you to see this as a 'Buying Signal'. So the answer, as per the training manual goes as follows: 'Sir, you do see great value in having a Xerox machine in your office and the benefits it will bring to your company. I appreciate your concern about the price of the machine. Let me explain how the machine will pay for itself in just a couple of years.'

One sure-fire way of achieving success is to be able to see rejections differently. Importantly, you should develop an ability to process 'mild rejections' and not let them defeat your spirits. Keep trying to meet the key decision-makers, by trying again and again. And if you don't get an appointment in spite of say ten attempts, go on for another ten, and another ten. But as we learnt from DK, if you ignore mild rejections, keep your spirit up, and keep trying, you too will succeed. And spring forward.

> **TAKEAWAY:** *Not all rejections are the same. Learn to process and decode the different shades of rejection. Develop your own ways of managing them differently.*

The Secrets of Start-Up Success

If people are not laughing at your goals,
your goals are too small.

—Azim Premji

You and your partner have worked on your dream project for more than a year. You have an excellent pitch deck ready. Your friends and well-wishers think you have a great business idea. You muster up enough courage and get a much treasured appointment with a respected venture capital firm. You present your idea with gusto. They smile, ask many polite questions then say that they will get back.

You never hear from them.

Now repeat this routine a hundred times over a span of 365 days.

After all these endless rejections, to the power of 100, you are able to smile and tell the story.

Meet Suhani Mohan and Karthik Mehta of Saral Designs. What I have narrated above is not a figment of my imagination, but something that Suhani and Karthik went through.

How did they manage to keep their sanity? How did they figure the way out of the maze?

Let me tell you a little about them and their company before I tell you about how they managed to process the rejection tsunami they faced.

Suhani Mohan is from an upper middle-class family from Mumbai and she was a very bright student right through school. She excelled in maths and science and so naturally her parents nudged her to take the IIT entrance exam. And she did manage to, as the young people are wont to saying 'crack the JEE'. She got into IIT Mumbai and her academic achievements did not wane once she entered IIT. She was a topper in her class, or a 'Nine Pointer' (the credit point system of the IITs was made famous by Chetan Bhagat through his book *Five Point Someone*). She had a very well-paying job in a leading MNC bank, but she was feeling restless. Within a year or two she was tired and bored with her job. She realised that her future calling was not in investment banking.

A chance application to join the Jagriti Yatra (a fifteen-day train trip through the poorer parts of India; you can learn more from www.jagritiyatra.com) got her to look at the lives of the less fortunate Indians. And in the process she started understanding the menstrual challenge being faced by the girls of the lower-income groups. She and her team managed to win the business plan competition at the end of the Jagriti Yatra. Her business concept was a low-cost machine to make a high-quality sanitary pad that could be sold at a much lower price than the MNC brands. As she reminisced, 'It is a lot easier to win a business plan competition than to actually create a running business.'

Karthik Mehta is from a business family and he too did his engineering from IIT Madras and landed a great job at General Motors. But he was more interested in designing machines than just operating them. He sought out a guru in the machine design domain, but that did not go far.

Suhani had set up her company at the IIT Mumbai Incubation Center, and Karthik literally stumbled upon her company as he went exploring for new ideas at the Incubation Center. They figured out they had complementary skills. Suhani was good at painting the big picture, Karthik loved working with and designing machines. They shook hands in December 2014 and launched their new company Saral Designs.

They managed to raise angel funds in May 2015, thanks to some connections in the IIT Mumbai ecosystem. The money they raised was enough to build a prototype of the sanitary pad machine and make a few thousand sanitary pads.

As they were getting ready to approach the VC community for their Series A funding, the entire ecosystem took a big hit. In March 2016, the VCs changed their agenda; from asking questions about 'how many downloads' 'how many new users', the question became 'what is the path to profit'. This sent every start-up that wanted a long-term view on funding into a tailspin. Saral Designs was no exception.

Suhani's presentation skills are indeed commendable. Using her IIT network she started making presentations to VCs. She recounted that she made a total of a hundred presentations to VCs between January and December 2016. A hundred!

The responses she got were almost parrot-like: 'You guys are amazing ... but...' She was ready for rejection, but what shocked her was the complete lack of feedback from VCs.

Thinking back, she says she got either total silence or just some very tangential useless ideas. And the VCs she met did not understand that she was not motivated by money alone. There was a larger cause, a larger problem she was trying to solve for the country.

As she was running short of funds she managed to find a mentor who ordered a machine, full cash down. She also got an order for a bulk shipment of sanitary napkins to Dubai.

But it was a hand-to-mouth existence right through the two years.

A meeting in Silicon Valley, where Suhani was invited to participate in a start-up bootcamp, changed her approach to pitching to VCs. The lady whom she met there said that Suhani was barking up the wrong tree. Investing in the manufacture of affordable sanitary pads and other such businesses aimed at the less fortunate is now termed 'Impact Investing', Suhani was told; and there were enough organisations and bodies that were keen on supporting such ventures. She was told to apply for grants from these global bodies. Over the next few months she managed to submit fifty applications and she bagged five grants. This was real money with no strings attached. No multiple spreadsheets. Imagine, 100 pitches to VCs got her zilch. And suddenly her strike rate jumps to 10 per cent.

Along the way she discovered that she should not have gone on with the endless charade of VC presentations. But she was hoping against hope that one of the frogs would turn out to be a prince. None did. One of the VCs got her to change her business (from making affordable pad-making machines to bulk manufacturing and marketing of branded pads), in an effort to quickly spin their investment into cash by selling to a potential investor. This set her back a full six months, burnt valuable cash and also made her hire and fire employees, something she was very upset about.

Suhani and Karthik, who set up their company in December 2014, have completed the fifth anniversary in December 2019. During the year 2018-19, they managed to figure out what they were all about: economical machines that can be used for a decentralised way of making high-quality yet economical sanitary napkins. They managed to garner grants, work with women's self-help groups and install a significant number of machines across India and Africa during the year. The next two years look good, but they are open for more challenges as they show up.

I asked Suhani and Karthik how they managed to face hundred rejections yet keep at it.

How did they process the rejection?

They said that they did not have a magic formula. They knew that there was always a Plan B and maybe a Plan C (they did feel that hiring and letting go employees during the up and down phases of the journey was the toughest to stomach). They knew that given their experience they could always land a job in a consulting company or elsewhere.

They felt that somewhere they knew that perseverance was a must to succeed in a journey such as theirs.

Small wins were a big morale booster for them; one big order from Dubai. A rupees five lakh fund infusion from an angel investor. A call from a customer who thanked them for doing such yeoman service for female empowerment.

The large Excel sheets that were created to track VC calls were changing from white to red (as VCs kept saying 'no'). In all this they felt that a few things helped them in their journey.

They spoke with their peers in the start-up ecosystem who were also struggling. If one looks at the start-up ecosystem, you will see that there are very few involved in hardcore engineering design and manufacturing. Many of the Indian start-ups are in the tech space. Then there are many in the e-commerce space: delivering beauty products to delivering food. But manufacturing is a rarity. At least in the popular start-up hubs. But they managed to speak to those involved in similar journeys and used those conversations to keep their spirits up. One such company that they truly admire is Ather Energy, the electric scooter company that was incubated in IIT Madras. Apparently, that company too went through many 'near-death' experiences.

Mentors and investors were yet another group that they were in touch with. Some of their early stage investors were themselves start-up entrepreneurs. They were a great sounding board to test out ideas. They were also there to provide encouraging words.

They point to their families for the complete support they received. One of them had to promise parents that this journey would not continue if they do not see light at the end of the tunnel by Day 1000. Again, parents had to be sensitised to the trials of a start-ups and the rejection journey they have to undertake.

They kept attending useful sessions. They recalled a session with Bunker Roy, the Padma Shri awardee and founder of the Barefoot College that works with rural communities to become self-sufficient. Bunker Roy told them that it would take a lifetime to effect change, and they were only on page one of chapter one of their journey.

Some days started with the thought 'Why get out of bed if I am going to get rejected again?'. But they kept telling themselves that 'Hope is the only medicine', 'Why focus on what is not in my control' and 'Let me focus on what is in my control'. They took time out to play football, to participate in competitions and even got excellent media coverage (Suhani appeared on the cover of *Forbes India* in a special issue that celebrated woman entrepreneurs).

I hope you get a broad idea of the journey they have had till now. They are clear that their journey is far from over. The dream is to get one machine working in every district of India (they were at ten at the last time we spoke). Then to have a machine in every district of Bangladesh, Sri Lanka and then every country in Africa. They are bound to hit new walls and face new shades of rejection. But they seem to have a formula that has worked for them. The same formula may work the next time. Or they may have to change the recipe and cook up a new magic potion.

Facing rejection is tough. But processing rejection is tougher still.

Psychologists tell us that it is better to take time to process the rejection instead of just brushing it aside with a smile. So don't sulk. But don't also brush it aside. Take it and process it carefully.

Suhani and Karthik kept focusing on what they still had in their life and did not let the rejections defeat them. They knew that they had a great education and every day they were gaining excellent new experience. All this would help them in whatever they would end up doing years later, they told themselves.

They managed to keep their self-confidence up. The endless VC questions and rejections did not dampen their spirits. Today they think back and say that they met a number of VCs who had no idea about how to evaluate their business plan. Many VCs they met only knew how to move numbers in an Excel spreadsheet. And Suhani must have made at least fifty versions of a five-year plan for such VCs.

Remember you need a friend and support group to be around you. You cannot make it alone. Decide who that will be. It could be a college friend. It could be a former colleague. Maybe a kind investor.

The rejection you received may not be about you at all. It is not personal. The person at the other end of the table may not have got what you were presenting. Or he got it all wrong.

With every rejection focus on what you can learn. Suhani, thinking back, says that she should have stopped after ten VC meetings and figured out that there was a big mismatch in what she was trying to do and what the VCs were looking for. She is thankful to the Silicon Valley lady to have cleared the fog that was clouding her vision. The same meeting, if it had happened a few months earlier, could have saved the Saral Designs team at least fifty useless presentations.

What I found was that right through this tough journey, Karthik and Suhani knew that they were going through a temporary phase. They were supremely confident in what they were doing and felt that if they kept at it they would succeed.

How about this one. As a school kid, Jack Andraka had a rather bizarre idea. What if he could create a test for pancreatic cancer that was better than what was available. A test that was 100 times better yet cost 26,000 times less. Everyone would clamour for the test, right? Well, 199 research labs rejected Andraka. Yes, 199. Finally, Johns Hopkins University accepted him and the test he developed is getting further refined as he enrolled for doing his undergraduate studies in Stanford University in 2018.

Is it that only new ideas and start-ups face rejections? A friend of mine in the Silicon Valley recounted this story. He has worked in the digital space for more than thirty years. He has created start-ups and sold them, several times. When we got talking he was working in a large company having sold his start-up to them. He was part of the senior management team and one of the tasks he had to do was to screen new ideas in the company for funding support. And what he found was indeed interesting. He felt that the company was full of people who would ask endless questions. So every new idea had to face multiple attacks. And since these ideas came from people who had a 'permanent' job in the company, most of the ideas were just destroyed in the meeting room.

The originators were not ready to stand up to the attackers and push for their idea

His observation was that, if he could take any of the ideas outside, work on the idea, build it up, he may have been be able to sell the same idea (as a start-up) to the same company for a multi-billion dollar valuation in a few years. We discussed how most companies are risk-averse and people are insecure about their own jobs. On the other hand, the start-up ecosystem, in the US and now in India, is built on the back of fearless, or you may call foolhardy, young and not-so-young people, who believe in the potential of their idea.

Now think about your own rejection journey. How are you processing the rejection you are getting?

Consider this thought experiment:

You have a B2B work profile but are keen on moving to a B2C company. You have excellent education and around five-year experience. You have applied to five jobs in B2C companies. And have not heard back from them. What will you do next?

Will you wait for them to respond? Or will you apply to five more companies? Or something else?

If you look at the to-do list above, you will probably be better off if you stop after five or ten and figure out where you are and where you can potentially be. Maybe you should be a little sad at the radio silence, but after grieving for a bit you need to get back into action mode.

What should you do?

What is your Rejection Processing System?

What is your first reaction to the rejection? Do you take it personally? Are you blaming something you cannot control for the rejection? What is the right response to the rejection? Do you have it figured out?

Once you have been rejected and have internalised it, grieved a bit, but not too much, what will you do next?

May be you should create your own think-tank support group to help you figure out a way to break into the B2C world. Whom will you reach out to? Do you have friends in some B2C companies who you can trust for sound judgement. You don't need people who will make polite noises.

You need people who can be brutally honest, yet constructive in their criticism

You also need people who can give you new pointers, like we saw with the startup entrepreneurs who were told to approach a different type of investors to break the 100-rejection jinx.

Taking time out to do something that will take your mind off the rejection syndrome is important when you are battling the rejection demon. So figure out what will re-energise you. Karthik plays football. What will help for you? Taking up swimming? Or learning to play the guitar?

Don't vent your anger on your near and dear ones. Don't post angst-filled messages on social media. Your family can be a great support system, just as they were for Suhani and Karthik.

Finally, be kind to yourself. You are successful in what you are doing. You need all the strength you have to go forward. So be kind. Be gentle yet demanding of your inner strength.

Sidharth Rao is the founder of the tremendously successful digital ad agency Webchutney. In his book *How I Almost Blew It*, he chronicles the many Indian startups who have had near-death experiences. He says, 'The media celebrates fundraising and other vanity milestones in a start-up's journey, adding to the perceptions that start-ups are romantic stories. In reality, they are difficult journeys fraught with hardships. In my twenty years in the start-up cosmos, I haven't encountered a single start-up that hasn't had a near-death experience, almost shut down, almost sold itself too short and, therefore almost "blew it".'

Today, Amazon is seen as so successful that there is an infographic that shows how Amazon wants to sell you everything, from food to books to movies. But Jeff Bezos met with a lot of questions on whether his enterprise would ever get going. In an interview with *60 Minutes*, he explained how he had to juggle many things in order to raise funds for his business: 'I had to take sixty meetings to raise $1 million and I raised it from twenty-two people at approximately $50,000 per person. It was nip and tuck whether I was going to be able to raise that money. So, the whole thing could have ended before the whole thing started. That was 1995, and the first question every investor asked me was, "*What is the internet?*".' But he survived to build one of the most successful global enterprises.

How do start-ups survive these near-death experiences? Obviously if you have the have the right RPS (Rejection Processing System), you can survive multiple rejections, near-death experiences and more.

Test your RPS the next time you are hit by a rejection. Whom can you reach out to? Who can help? Who can give you honest feedback? See if it helps you to bounce back. If not, it is time for you to create an all-new RPS. Remember that you can spring back and spring forward only if you have a robust Rejection Processing System.

TAKEAWAY: *Just because you have faced multiple rejection does not mean that you will not achieve success. Remember the importance of a good rejection processing system. Seek out new mentors who can guide you out of the multiple rejection scenario.*

Rescued by the Rejection Résumé

*You must first be willing to fail … and you must have the courage
to go for it anyhow.*

—Michael Bloomberg

Imagine this. You have had an excellent five years of experience in sales. Having done your MBA, you bravely opted for a sales job. You took on a challenging territory as the Territory Manager and achieved a remarkable turnaround. That led to a better posting and then, an even better posting. You have completed five years in sales and it is not sure to you if the company you are working for would move you to marketing or operations or any other role. So you have started looking around and an old friend working with a good company refers you to his HR Head. And you are at the interview.

You have prepared well for the interview. And you have excellent answers for all the standard questions: What are your top three achievements? What are your strengths? What are your weaknesses? Why do you want to move to marketing? Why are you not requesting your current company to give you a marketing job? Will you really want to leave your current employer? Who was your favourite boss and why? What was the most challenging job you have done till date?

Then comes a question that you did not prepare for: *Tell us about three of your biggest rejections or failures.* What did you learn from them?

I have had the opportunity of interviewing candidates who brazenly say they have not had any rejection or failure in their work life. This always sets alarm bells ringing in my head. There are candidates who sheepishly say that they failed to achieve some small job (the ppt had a few spelling mistakes and that was pointed out by the boss) and the failure was not something that they were too worried about. Again, alarm bells.

The person interviewing you knows that you are not a superman or a superwoman. You must have failed or been rejected on several occasions. Why is it that you are not able to speak about your rejections and failures? What is holding you back? The question serves several important purposes. Are you willing to admit that you were rejected or failed, sometimes spectacularly? After you failed, did you introspect why you failed? What lessons did you learn from the rejection? How will you do the job better the next time?

Let us play this out. You are asked, 'Tell me about a big failure you had and why it happened and what have you learnt?'

You say that you failed to get into the top-selling territory merit list in your company. And that was because one big distributor decided to cancel a big order at the last minute. You had no time to compensate for your loss. The lesson learnt is that never wait for the last minute to fulfill your target. Plan in advance and ensure that all the ducks are in a row, before you take a shot.

That was a simple story. May serve the purpose. Definitely better than saying that you have not faced any major rejection.

What if your story was a lot more interesting? Something a coachee shared with me.

The biggest failure you had was the inability to work with a top sales executive. You never got his respect and in turn he did not follow your orders. Not that he was a bad apple. He was possibly the best sales executive in the whole region. He never really accepted you as his 'boss' and in a sense he rejected your authority to oversee his performance. By not having him fully aligned, you could not use him to the best of his capabilities. You underestimated his ability to resist your powers and you overestimated the position power you had. Thinking back, you approached the problem from the wrong end. You did not put yourself in his shoes, when you as a twenty-four-year-old freshly minted MBA became his boss. May be the fifth he has had in his fifteen-year career. And you never got his respect and regard.

How could you have processed this better?

You could have reached out to someone senior in the company for advice, early in the game. You did not do that and allowed the situation to worsen and the wound to fester. If you had got some good mentoring help as the situation was developing, you may have been able to get the super sales guy to execute your plans the way you wanted them done. (in the case of my coachee, she managed to discuss the problem with her coach and understood what she was doing was wrong). In fact, you could have used him as a sounding board for your new ideas, may be use him to train the sales executives who were struggling. Many missed opportunities.

To me, the second story sounds a lot more credible. A lot more insightful. And as a HR manager, I would have loved to get into a deeper discussion on people management and how top performers are always more difficult to manage.

That is just one example of a failure and how you managed to learn from the failure.

Tim Herrera in his blog post in the *New York Times* titled 'Do you keep a Failure Résumé?' points to a new phenomenon that seems to be gaining currency, the 'Failure Résumé' or the 'Rejection Résumé'. Our résumés are always filled with glorious things we have accomplished and when asked we speak of our successes and how we achieved all that through better preparation, better delegation, better planning and so on. But failing or getting rejected gives us an important opportunity to see what went wrong, the traits we have that lead to our failure and that is an opportunity that we should embrace. While your standard résumé captures your successes, your failure résumé tracks the occasions and incidents when you did not hit the mark.

The concept of the failure résumé gained currency after Melanie Stefan of the University of Edinburgh published her 'CV of Failures' in the journal *Nature*. This short article has been referred to by many leading academics as a way of capturing the struggle and challenge that is part-and-parcel of an academic life. Stefan wrote that creating a failure résumé '… will probably be utterly depressing at first sight. But it will remind you of the missing truths, some of the essential parts of what it means to be a scientist—and it might inspire a colleague to shrug off a rejection and start again'.

Taking inspiration from Prof. Stefan, Johannes Haushofer an assistant professor of psychology at Princeton University displayed his 'CV of Failures' on his personal website. He writes in his cover note: 'Most of what I try fails, but these failures are often invisible, while the successes are visible. I have noticed that this sometimes gives others an impression that most things work out for me. As a result, they are more likely to attribute their own failures to themselves.'

A rejection tells us a lot about ourselves and how we are wired

Do we take the rejection and blame it on others? Or do we take the rejection as a sign that we need to get better?

Carol Dwek in her best-selling must-read book *Mindset: The New Psychology of Success* describes two types of internal wiring we all have. The first is what she calls a 'fixed, indset'. Those with a fixed mindset believe that their abilities are inherited and immutable. The others have what she calls the 'growth mindset'. These people believe that their abilities such as intelligence and creativity can be developed through time, from practice and learning.

Prof. Dwek says that praising children for accomplishments alone for seemingly stable traits produces a fixed mindset: 'You are really talented. You draw so well. You are a natural painter.' This gets the kids' wiring to align and believe that they have these inherent traits. She says that growth mindset can be developed by praising both the effort and the achievement: 'Your efforts are really paying off. I am sure you will continue to get better and better. Don't stop trying.' On doing this, kids start developing an attitude that it is good to try things and test their abilities. They will get praised even if they fail, because they took the effort to try. Praising the kid for his effort gives her a programme to follow right through her life. While praising the kid for ability alone gives no clue on how to modify behaviour.

Our workplaces are modelled to create fixed mindset robots

If you achieve your budget, you get your bonus. If you miss the numbers, you don't make the bonus.

Corporations that want to create a growth mindset among its employees need to create a culture of learning, feedback and intelligent risk-taking. And embrace failure or rejection. Coaching, training, leadership development programmes and tuition reimbursements are the norms in some of these corporations.

You can test your own mindset at Carol Dwek's website www.mindsetworks.com. I suppose you need to create a test of this sort for companies too to figure out which company encourages a fixed mindset and which one looks for and rewards a growth mindset.

A good indicator is how the managers in the company look at rejection. Is it seen as a permanent black mark on your CV? Or is it seen as an important milestone and a good learning experience? This attitude may also get reflected in the way they ask questions of a fresh recruit. I would submit that companies with a risk-taking mindset would want to know your failures and what you learnt from them, and not just stick to asking the clichéd questions about your success and your strengths.

You have a CV which lists your achievements. And possibly you have revised it every time you got promoted or got a new assignment. Here is an important question:

Do you have a Rejection Résumé?

Have you considered creating one? This is a résumé for your own personal use and reflection. In this résumé, list the rejections you have had to face. Prof. Haushofer listed the papers that got rejected by reviewers, the grant applications that got turned down. And his own reflection of why these rejections happened.

A rejection résumé or a failure résumé is not just for the academics. Even in corporate life, we can learn a lot by going through our own rejection résumé. As the famous old saying goes, 'A genius learns from others' mistakes. An intelligent man learns from his own mistakes. A fool never learns.'

As you go through your rejection résumé you will discover that some patterns are repeating themselves: You give up too early. You present your ideas without giving them deeper thought. You are a lone ranger, you don't involve your colleagues or associates when you pitch new ideas. You are impatient with your response and damage your chances just about when the tide is turning.

The rejection résumé will also show you if you are endowed with a fixed mindset or a growth mindset. I suspect that the mere process of creating a rejection résumé means that you are on your way to developing a growth mindset.

Thomas Alva Edison has been described as America's greatest inventor. Among other things he invented electric power generation, motion pictures, mass communication and sound recording. The devices he invented include the movie camera and the light bulb, a device that probably contributed to the development of human kind more than any other single device. He did not succeed in all that he tried to do. He is said to have observed: 'I have not failed. I have just found 10,000 ways that won't work.' And: 'Many of life's failures are people who didn't realise how close they were to success before they gave up.'

I am sure Thomas Edison had a fascinating rejection résumé. And he benefitted from his mistakes.

Through the course of the book you would have noticed I have referred to several of my own rejection stories and what I learnt from them. Failing to get into Hindustan Lever, twice. Failing to win a coveted Korean car account (this is in the upcoming chapter). A leading international professor rejecting my idea of a book on Indian advertising cases. Taking on a task for which I was least prepared as I flew to Kochi. I could add a few more: not successful in setting up a pre-press outsourcing unit; my article getting rejected by an important journal; a brand launch that got rejected by the consumers and so many more.

I have done my bit of reflecting on my rejections. And these reflections helped me plan my future better.

It's time you considered creating a rejection résumé of your own.

> **TAKEAWAY:** *If you can accept and process rejection, you will no longer hide your rejection and failures. Once you are ready to face the rejection and handle them, your ability to spring back will improve. And your self-development gets a boost when you are able to wear rejection like a badge of honour.*

part three

LEARNING AND PROGRESSING POST REJECTION

Spring designing is a complex process. It is an iterative process which may require several iterations before the best design is achieved.

—Standard Handbook of Machine Design

Finishing is the third step in the making of a spring. The ends go through grinding and polishing, making it ready for use.

A Well-Learnt Driving Lesson

Rejection is nothing more than a necessary step
in the pursuit of success.

—Bo Bennet, social psychologist,
author and entrepreneur

If any ad agency veteran tells you that their agency won every new business pitch they participated in, take it with not a pinch, but with a ton of salt. The same could be said of a merchant banker who claims that they won every IPO mandate they pitched for. Or an IT Services firm that claims that they won every RFP they responded to.

In my own life I have won some great new business pitches (you will hear of them in various parts of this chapter) and I have had some disasters. And the story that follows is about how a disastrous pitch led to some serious introspection and to a bigger win.

The mid-1990s was a great time to be in Indian marketing services business. With the opening up of the Indian economy we saw the entry of many new companies. From a command- and supply-driven economy India transitioned in less than a decade into a demand- and consumer-driven economy.

Products for which you had to wait for months and years for delivery became available off-the-counter. Limited choices in televisions, washing machines, computers, two-wheelers and many other products soon became a thing of the past. Exciting things began to take place in the automobile sector. It was once said that 5 per cent of the US economy (and employment) depended in some form or the other on the automotive sector. The opening up of the Indian auto sector and the entry of new companies spelt big opportunities for ad agencies and media firms.

Ulka Advertising, the Indian agency where I worked transitioned into FCB Ulka, a part of the Foote Cone Belding global network in 1997. Unlike many of its cohorts, Ulka did not have the benefit of large MNC accounts such as Unilever, P&G, Nestle, Coke, Pepsi, Colgate and IBM. And we knew that FCB was not in a position to give us large accounts. Therefore, we had to pretty much do our own 'hunting'.

One interesting factoid that stood out when we scanned the global advertising markets was the importance of automobile brands. In most countries at least a few automobile brands were among the top ten advertisers. In India, given the virtual monopoly Maruti enjoyed, the advertising of automobiles was just a drop, compared to the ocean of advertising unleashed by the soap and detergent brands.

The first set of international automobile companies to enter India were Ford (with Ford Escort) and GM (with Opel Astra). Soon to follow was Mitsubishi Lancer and Daewoo Cielo. We did not win any of these accounts but were sure that many more interesting brands would follow these. Anyway, Ford and GM were not approachable since they were aligned globally with their ad agencies.

In the middle of all this, we heard Hyundai was going to enter India and soon enough we got a call from Mr B.V.R. Subbu, a Tata Motors (then known as TELCO) veteran, who was joining the Korean major as head of operations. We studied the brief given; it was for the launch of a sedan in the Indian market. The pitch was slated for the next month. We did some consumer research, created a few speculative campaigns and landed up in Chennai for the pitch. Hyundai was setting up a state-of-the art factory in Tamil Nadu and at that time they were planning on even having their Corporate and Marketing headquarters in Chennai. Several agencies had been invited for the pitch and we were one of them.

When your pitch goes well, you realise it during the pitch itself. If not during the pitch, immediately after you know how well you did. In this case, we knew we did not make a good impression. We blew the pitch. And were ready to be 'rejected' even before we got into the aircraft for our flight back to Mumbai.

As we got back to Mumbai, we started digging deeper into why we felt that we would get rejected. Did we not do enough homework? Was our strategy wrong? Were the creatives we presented not up to the mark? Or was it a combination of all these?

One thing we realised was that winning a car account was not going to be easy. And our level of preparation was woefully inadequate.

We heard a few weeks later a smaller agency had won the Hyundai pitch, much against the predictions of some of our own experts. Obviously, they had done something that impressed a car veteran like B.V.R. Subbu.

Stop here and think for a bit.

What to do when you are rejected?

We were rejected. We did not indulge in blaming the client for partiality or bias. There were enough reasons for bias: we were an Indian agency with no real automotive experience, we did not know B.V.R. Subbu well nor did we know any of his colleagues at Hyundai, we had no Korean connection, we had no global knowledge about the auto sector and so on.

What would be the lessons you would have taken back after that rejection? What would you do next?

Unlike in a job hunt, where you can apply to the same company after a few months for a different job, in the case of a new business hunt, an opportunity lost is gone for at least a few years (though this is decreasing as we speak).

What do you think we should have done?

Just as you celebrate after each win, it is important that you introspect after every rejection

This should be an established practice, if you want to learn from each of your failures and rejection.

The internal after-action-review pointed to several flaws in the way we approached the pitch. We had treated the pitch as yet another run-of-the-mill pitch. We had done a little bit of homework and created communication programmes. We also realised that we need to get into a different mode if we were to land the next big auto account that would come up for a pitch.

Adam Grant, an American psychologist and a professor in organisational psychology at Wharton Business School, University of Pennsylvania, in his highly engaging podcast on

'How to Bounce Back From Rejection' tells us a story about how his papers got rejected several times with rather strong comments from reviewers. After one such rejection, he decided to go into an overdrive and worked continuously for five days to redraft the rejected paper and resubmitted it to the reputed journal. The paper got accepted and apparently, the editor commented that he was accepting the paper partly because it is of acceptable quality but also because he was impressed at the way Adam managed to get back on his feet after such a bad rejection. Prof. Grant says that he discovered the power of not just bouncing back, but *bouncing forward*. So when you get rejected you can wallow in self-pity and blame the world. A much better way out would be to spring back into your normal state. Even better is what Prof. Grant prescribes: bounce forward.

Now let me tell you how we managed to 'bounce forward'. Or 'spring forward'.

We had lost the Hyundai pitch. But we had lost the battle, not the war. We realised that many more companies would be launching cars and we had to be ready to go after them, maybe even before they sent out an RFP. Soon enough we read the glowing reports of Tata's new car which was unveiled at the Auto Expo 1998. We had missed going to the Auto Expo but knew that Tata Motors was yet to invite agencies for a pitch. The car, then called 'Project Mint' got some rave reviews from media as well as from the then industries minister of the government of India.

We started figuring out how we could get in touch with Tata Motors and begin engaging with them on the new car launch.

Management consultants, marketing services companies and ad agencies have interesting ways of engaging with potential clients. We had created a marketing communication (MarCom) case study competition, FCB Ulka Comstrat, in partnership with a leading business school in Mumbai. The idea was to request a client organisation to give us a real-life MarCom case, which is then given out to B-Schools all over India. The submissions are shortlisted by a panel of agency experts. The shortlisted B-Schools, five or six of them, are invited to Mumbai for the final presentation in front of a jury consisting of a representative from the client organisation and the agency team. Comstrat was started in 1995 and was in its third year in 1998. We realised that Comstrat could be a very good door-opener for us to engage with Tata Motors on their new car launch well before the RFPs were sent out. Importantly, the intended launch of the new Tata car could make an interesting real-life MarCom case study to give to the B-Schools.

A few phone calls later we met with the marketing team at Tata Motors and explained the concept behind Comstrat. The client was not willing to share any confidential information, as is always the case. We explained that we would write the case based on whatever information that was freely available in public domain. They only had to okay the short case write-up. We also requested the Head of Marketing, Mr S Krishnan that it would be a good morale booster for the students if he could be there at the final presentations. Krishnan, being a B-School graduate himself readily agreed.

As we were winding down the meeting, Mr Krishnan asked us an interesting question: 'Does your agency handle any automotive accounts?' We said that our Delhi office had a small part of Hindustan Motors (HM) account (Contessa brand) but we were keen on finding out what he had in mind. Mr Krishnan explained that Tata Motors worked with Rediffusion for their commercial vehicles and corporate advertising, but would be looking out for an agency partner for their new small car project. He said that they could consider us if we were willing to drop HM from our portfolio, if in case we got selected. We replied that we would discuss the matter internally and get back. Mr Krishnan left us with an interesting point to ponder over: 'Remember Tata Motors will one day be your biggest account if you win. You can take it from me!'

The Comstrat competition went well and the final presentations were well-received by the team from Tata Motors.

Soon after the Comstrat Competition, we were invited by Tata Motors for a formal briefing on the new car. The name 'Tata Indica' was finalised much later. The brief was quite skeletal and we were asked to do our own research to fill out the empty slots in the brief. One thing that stood out was that the new car would be available in both petrol and diesel variants.

In the 1990s, diesel cars had a bad reputation. They were seen as big polluters, oil-guzzlers and a big pain to maintain. The only small diesel cars on the road were taxis and they were noisy, belching out black smoke as they traversed the roads of Mumbai and other big cities.

As we started digesting the brief we also started speaking with some consumer behaviour experts. Some of them gave Tata Motors very little chance of success. The deck was stacked against Tata according to them: new entrant in cars, noisy commercial vehicle expertise is different from car expertise, who wants a small diesel car, and the list of negatives could go on.

We had two months to mount the presentation (if you count the days we worked on the Comstrat case, we had a few more weeks to live with the brand communication problem). We had learnt our lesson from the Hyundai rejection. We wanted to 'bounce forward' or 'spring forward' as Prof. Grant would say today.

The first step we undertook was to see how diesel cars were perceived in other parts of the world. And our research revealed that while diesel cars were virtually non-existent in the USA, they accounted for almost 40 per cent of all cars sold in Europe. Why? Simply because fuel costs (both petrol and diesel) in continental Europe were significantly higher than in USA. Intrinsically, diesel engines are more fuel-efficient, hence in Europe they enjoyed great popularity, in spite of diesel models being a little more expensive. Obviously, the diesel engines sold in Europe were not the noisy, oil-guzzling, smoke-belching monsters, we had been witnessing on Indian roads. Clearly, there was a lot more to small diesel cars than what we had imagined.

In India, a diesel car would also have the price advantage of diesel fuel, which was subsidised since it was largely used in goods transport. So if you combine the lower price of diesel and the higher fuel efficiency of a diesel engine, a small diesel car, of acceptable quality, priced rightly, could be a big success. We started developing our own confidence in the Tata Motors proposition.

How about consumers? What would they say?

We had Dorab Sopariwala, the psephologist and the former joint managing director of Indian Market Research Bureau and the founder of MARG Research as our strategy advisor. This was a good problem to pose to him, I thought.

Dorab saw the data we had at our disposal about the car, its shape, engine capacity, interior space, petrol/diesel options etc. On deeper reflection his suggestion was that we could test the importance of various attributes by doing a conjoint analysis research with consumers. Conjoint analysis was developed as a way of getting consumers to look at product options with multiple attributes. For example, if we took five attributes (size, fuel efficiency, shape, price, compay reputation) and each had three values, we would end up with several hundred options. Conjoint simplifies the number of options to be placed in front of the consumer. Based on their response, we could identify what were the weightages that consumer assigned to each of the attributes. So for example, you might find that consumers gave greater weight to fuel efficiency than size.

The conjoint analysis revealed some interesting facts. Unlike the marketing gurus, an average car buyer gave Tata high scores and they also gave diesel high scores. We realised that Tata needed to build on their strengths and instead of being defensive, they had to get aggressive with their offering.

In addition to a deep dive into consumer and consumer understanding and developing a variety of advertising creatives, we also wanted to present our own 360-degree approach to auto car branding. So we created a complete customer relationship programme kit for the new car.

It turned out that we were the first ad agency to present to the Tata Motors team. While we had met Mr Krishnan before, it was the first time we met the head of the passenger vehicles business, Mr Rajiv Dube. The presentation started at 5 p.m. and went on till 9 p.m., if I remember correctly.

In the agency selection process, the old lesson is to go first or to go last. Maybe going first was a blessing for us. Tata Motors decided to invite all agencies who had shown interest in the business. I was told that not less than fourteen agencies presented over a span of two months.

When the results were announced, we had won the business. Hands down. An insider told us that after our presentation, which was so comprehensive, it was a downward ride all the way.

Let us now get back to what we are trying to understand here: how to recover from a rejection and get better or spring forward at what we are doing?

The best way to handle a rejection, any rejection, is to see how we can learn from the rejection and spring forward

In 1975, Anna Wintour was fired from her position as fashion editor at *Harper's Bazaar* magazine, just nine months after she had been hired. But it turned out to be a blessing according to Wintour. In the book *Winners*, she told the author Alistair Campbell: 'Everyone should get sacked at least once. It forces you to look at yourself… It is important to have setbacks, because that is the reality of life. Perfection does not exist.' Wintour is today the unanointed queen of high fashion and has been the editor-in-chief of *Vogue* for over thirty years. In fact, the movie *Devil Wears Prada*, where Meryl Streep essayed the role of a diva editor, is supposed to have been based on Wintour and her style of working. From being fired to becoming an icon. That is Anna Wintour's rejection story.

Think back to a time you got rejected. It may have been for a plum assignment. Or it may be a proposal you presented to your board. Or it may have been for a job interview.

You face rejection. What do you do now?

In this story you were shown what happens when you get up from your rejection with a new resolve to 'spring forward'. Not just bounce out of the rejection, but to actively engage in moving forward.

In his book *Antifragile*, Nassim Nicholas Taleb, the bestselling author says, 'Some things benefit from shocks; they thrive and grow when exposed to volatility, randomness, disorder, and stressors, and love adventure, risk and uncertainty.' Yet, in spite of the ubiquity of the phenomenon, there is no word for the exact opposite of fragile. According to Taleb, the opposite of fragile is antifragile. Antifragility is beyond resilience or robustness. The resilient resists shocks and stays the same; the antifragile gets better. My usage of the concept of 'antifragile' maybe out of context. But my intention is to ask when you get rejected, can you use the rejection to become stronger?

As children, we did it naturally. We fell down, we stumbled. We got up and started walking again. If an adult was observing us, we cried … maybe! If not, we were on our feet soon enough, a little stronger than we were before we fell.

Why should it be any different when you face rejection in your adult life? Why should a rejection lead to a deep sense of discomfort and self-doubt?

You cannot dial back the time clock. What has happened has happened. You cannot keep lamenting the fact that you should have prepared better for the interview. Or the fact that your presentation should have had better graphics. Or that you should have done better homework before entering the meeting. All that is water under the bridge.

What can you learn from the rejection? Instead of getting into self-flagellation, can you systematically diagnose what you did right and what you did wrong? What could you have done better? What can you learn from what just happened?

It is from there that you will obtain the seeds for your 'bounce forward' or 'spring forward' strategy. It is possible that you had not prepared well enough for your interview. Maybe your dress was all wrong. The next time what are you going to do? Will you read up more? Will you speak to some domain experts (remember without Dorab's inputs we would not have figured out the way to use conjoint analysis)? Will you invest in learning more about what is important?

Play the other rejection story. Your proposal just got rejected by your superiors. What could you have done better? Maybe met with them and sounded them out before making a final pitch?

Finally, you need to remember rejection is not the end of the road. Sometimes a rejection can lead to so many new learnings that you may end up in a better place.

To complete the Hyundai and Tata Motors story, the agency that won the Hyundai account did great work but did not get to work with Hyundai for more than six or seven years. The Korean company brought their own agency Innocean Worldwide to India to handle the brand advertising, once their business began to do well. In contrast, Tata Motors has stayed with FCB Ulka from 1998 till the date this book was going into print. A whopping twenty-two years and counting. And for more than a decade it was the flagship account for the agency. So the 'spring forward' strategy paid off very well indeed.

> **TAKEAWAY:** *Every rejection is a learning opportunity. Don't let a rejection destroy your enthusiasm. Learn from the rejection and get better the next time. Don't waste your time playing the blame game or giving excuses.*

Bureaucracy's Rejection—in Triplicate

You may not realise it when it happens, but a kick in the teeth
may be the best thing in the world for you.

—Walt Disney

Shailaja Chandra, the Chief Secretary of the Delhi government, writing in connection with the seventy-fifth anniversary of independent India (in the *Hindustan Times* dated 12 June 2019) said '… new laws, reforms and announcements can be expected. Will a risk-averse, status-quoist bureaucracy rise to the occasion? Will the Indian Adminstrative Service (IAS) bureaucrats mostly posted in the states become agents of transformation or *(will they)* find ways to stonewall change?'

The Indian bureaucracy, a legacy of the British Raj, is often called the 'steel frame' that keeps India together. It is also in equal measure blamed for its fondness for rules and regulations, miles of red tape, need for triplicate copies of everything and blamed for tying the country up in knots (the article written by a former bureaucrat quoted above is a proof in point).

***But do bureaucrats too have their share of rejection?
And how do they handle it?***

I posed this question to a former bureaucrat who served in the IAS for several decades.

In his view, bureaucrats in the Indian system face two types of rejection. The first set of rejection are those they face when they start out, early in their career. These rejections are often faced before they complete five years in the government service and are very difficult to handle. Some of them wonder if they will lose their job (they will not), some lament their relative lack of success compared to their 'batchmates'. So they start looking for options both inside and outside the government. Today, most IAS recruits are highly qualified; many of them have a professional degree—engineering, MBA etc. And they pick up a good job outside in a jiffy. Since most of them are double-income households, the pain of transition is not too difficult to handle.

The second type of rejection happens right through their career, for the next twenty-five-plus years. These rejections could be of different types.

Rejection in the government can be as simple as not being invited for a meeting. In the corporate sector, this may not be seen as a rejection. But in the government, it is noticed by everyone including the peon and all the clerical staff in the office. And as you walk into the office the following day, you may get sympathetic nods from everyone in the office including the junior-most staff. I am not sure this happens in corporate India.

The second type of rejection is that which is handed out to a proposal you may have championed. In the bureaucracy proposals that are put up by someone lower down are routinely rejected by someone higher up. Often a proposal from one department is rejected by another department for the simple fact they did not think of it first, or as as an unwarranted departmental overreach. You may not get a logical explanation for the rejection after the meeting. Imagine you are the bureaucrat looking after the sanitation department in a state and have some good ideas to implement. Your proposals, in the government system, may not make much headway. It goes into the famous black hole of Indian bureaucracy. There is no way you can seek clarification or try and present it with a fancy PowerPoint in a board room (this will happen soon, I suppose). You keep slogging at your day job and get on with your next big idea on say potable water supply to the shantytowns of the metropolis.

The third type of rejection is not being selected for interesting and rewarding assignments. In the government service, as you move higher, you could get a chance to work around the world. But you may not get your chance at all. And if you don't get your chance by the time you complete twenty years in the system, you may never get a chance. You may never know why you were not recommended. It could be that you were not liked by the powers-that-be. Or you were held back by your current boss. Or your name was sent as a back-up, and the first name got picked all the time. So you were always a bridesmaid, but never the bride.

Government bureaucracies around the world behave similarly and have their own languge codes. Nothing captured it better than the highly popular BBC Series, *Yes Minister* and *Yes Prime Minister*. An article that appeared in *The Telegraph* presented the ten most famous scenes from the series.

I found one particularly amusing.

When the Minister is inundated with correspondence, Sir Bernard offers to take it off his hands by sending 'official replies'.

> Sir Bernard: 'I'll just say, "The Minister has asked me to thank you for your letter" and something like "the matter is under consideration", or even "under active consideration".'

> Minister Jim Hacker: 'What's the difference?'

> Sir Bernard: 'Well, "under consideration" means we've lost the file, "under active consideration" means we're trying to find it.'

I do hope the above exchange was just a figment of the writer's imagination.

Anil Swarup, former Union Coal and Education Secretary writing in the *Hindu Business Line* (20 June 2019) points out to two new developments in the Indian civil services. The increase in the admission age of IAS which happened a decade or two ago, and the move towards lateral recruitments into government service. He feels that the increase in entry age has created a syndrome of 'hard boiled eggs' who are difficult to train (and who take rejections more severely). Lateral entrants may create a new set of problems unless officers are asked to mentor the new entrants (both lateral and new IAS officers), closely at least for the first few years. While complimenting the selection process and the wonderful institutions that are being run largely by IAS officers, such as the Election Commission and the Union Public Service Commission (UPSC), Anil Swarup says that there needs to be a serious reorientation of the civil service since evaluations (that can also be reinterpreted as rejection) are '… opaque and have had a demoralising effect on the civil service'.

If you are one of the smart ones to have got into IAS, IFS or IPS or any one of the other Indian government services, are you prepared to face rejection which are going to be part of your daily routine?

Will you cow down to the system or bravely work for the larger cause?

T.N. Seshan who passed away on 10 November 2019 was an IAS officer who chose his own path. The youngest of six siblings born in a middle-class family, he joined the IAS in 1954 and was posted in the Tamil Nadu cadre in 1955. He was appointed as a Transport Secretary in the Tamil Nadu government, and when taunted by the unions on what he knew about a bus, he decided to learn bus driving and repair. Once he even chastised a bus driver who was driving rashly, took over the steering wheel of the bus and delivered the eighty passengers to their destination, safely. He served across multiple departments spanning the Department of Atomic Energy, Environment and Forests, Ministry of Defence and was also Cabinet Secretary. He was the Chief Election Commissioner from December 1990 to December 1996. It was here he left a permanent mark on the democratic fabric of our country. When he spotted widespread vote rigging and impersonation of voters he insisted that voters be given an individual voter ID. This proposal was roundly rejected by many political parties. But he held on to his guns insisting that from January 1995, no election would take place without the voter ID. And his steadfast commitment to this objective worked. The Supreme Court stepped in to support his call for a voter ID. Today, all of us carry a voter ID when we head to cast our vote. And we can thank the late T.N. Seshan for this privilege. So inspite of getting rejected multiple times, his persistence paid off and we remember him as one of our true heroes.

For a start you need to realise that getting into the IAS is only the beginning and it is not the end of the race

The rat race really starts after you get in. You may say this is true in every sphere of life, be it corporate India or the professional services etc. But in the government services, it is widely believed that once you make the IAS you are made for life. That unfortunately is not true. So as you celebrate your successful attempt at getting the much sought-after IAS tag, you need to be ready to face rejections and problems. Remember that it is a thirty-five-year race and some breaks will turn out okay in the long run. In fact, you are the most vulnerable in the early stages of your career and you need to figure out how you will cope with rejection during your initial days/years. In your later years, you would have developed your coping mechanism to handle it. You need your rejection processing system up and running all the time.

While the government system is often opaque, but to succeed in your career as a bureaucrat you need to figure out where the levers of power lie. Who are the decision-makers? Who are the influencers? And who is advising them? You should be able to understand the internal dynamics.

As I was told, a senior IAS officer was posted to a position in a public-sector unit (PSU) that needed the government's oxygen support. When his first term, which was for just one year, was complete, the government changed (i.e., the party in power changed) and the new minister was given some wrong advice that made him restrict the extension to just one more year. A personal meeting with the minister ended up clearing the air and a two-year term was given. This extended stay in that position opened up new avenues for growth for this IAS officer. He went on to head up larger and larger undertakings and then reinvented himself as a much-in-demand independent director on some of the most sought after corporate boards. If he had accepted the one-year extension, he would have been called back to Delhi and may have ended up in a dead-end job, near the end of his career. Instead, he managed to cap his career with some tremendous achievements and awards, that led to more doors being opened for his future growth and gainful employment.

Very rarely in government service do you go up to your boss and demand something. At least in the IAS one could come to grief if the discussion spun out of control and went the wrong way. But in the case above, the discussion opened up new avenues for growth. The key learning is to weigh the odds and see what would be the best way forward: staying silent and keeping the nose to the grindstone, or trying your chance at a face-to-face meeting. You need to take the call quickly if you want a decision changed.

The government bureaucracy has its own ways of handing out a rejection. And there are many ways it is done as a seasoned bureaucrat may tell you.

A business school was in a quandary. They were struggling with their campus expansion plans when they received a formal letter from the governor of a large State requesting them to set up a new campus in that (neighbouring) state. The state government was offering a huge swathe of land in one of the better cities of that large state. Gratis. As the B-School was wondering how to respond, they had a visitor from that state's industrial development department who wanted to present the case with the management for the campus in his state. In the detailed discussions it emerged that there was a land-grab game in the offing and the B-School was a tool in a larger game.

How could the B-School reject the offer? It was here that the unique rejection playbook system of the Indian bureaucracy came to their help. One of the advisors of the B-School was a retired senior bureaucrat. He told the B-School not to worry but refer the matter in all sincerity to the relevant government department in Delhi. He said they would decode the many messages and respond. And if they, through their own system, found out that the offer was not 'kosher' they would just go silent on the issue (the matter would perhaps be under 'active consideration' as Sir Bernard would have said). That would be a good enough reason for the B-School to politely ignore the offer. Chances were that in time, the government would change in that state and this scheme get buried in one of the files. To complete the story, this is exactly what happened. After the matter was referred to Delhi, it found a decent burial. No more letters or visits. Technically, the B-School had done its duty and was now in the clear, without really rejecting any offer.

So referring the matter to a higher authority is a commonly used method of rejection. There are many other methods of rejection in government service: referring it to a different department, citing a past violation, going back to the rule book, seeking a clarification and finally setting up a committee to look into it. For those of us interested in knowing the way the bureaucracy works, as I have mentioned earlier, nothing is better than watching the BBC Series *Yes Minister* and *Yes Prime Minister*. While the BBC series may have exaggerated to prove a point and to tickle your funny bone, there was probably some truth in all the Machiavellian moves that were shown in the series. Truth be told, rejection in the government service comes in many shades and it is often done very smoothly.

If you are in the government, the biggest lesson is that you need to plan your thirty-year journey, as soon as you complete your first five years. You will get numerous rejections along the way, but you must not let them destroy you. Take them in your stride and move onwards.

You can reduce the severity of the rejection into a simpler 'setback'. In your own mind, you need to see when a rejection becomes a 'REJECTION' and when it is just a 'setback'.

The more successful bureaucrats manage to figure out this formula early in their career. Some of them complete a full career in the government and then go for one more inning as corporate advisors. Some of them move to government undertakings and build a career in the industry or service sector. One thing is common to all of them, they manage their rejections very well.

The lessons learnt from the IAS are applicable to all forms of government services: IPS, IFS and more. The shades of rejection may vary, but in all the government services, there are various forms of rejection to be handled. So if you are in the private sector and think that things are rosy in the 'permanent' government job, please wake up. The grass is not really that much greener on the other side.

So how do you rebound after a career setback, in private sector or in the government?

In the article in *Harvard Business Review* (October 2014) 'Rebounding from Career Setbacks', authors Mitchell Lee Marks, Philip Mirvis and Ron Ashkenas quote psychiatrist Elisabeth Kubler-Ross on how people manage career setbacks. Kubler-Ross says that we work ourselves through some classic stages of loss. Firstly, we are in shock and in a state of denial about the events. We move from this stage to a sense of anger at the company and the boss. We then move to a protracted stage of licking our wounds and wondering if we will ever be able to regain the respect and regard of the peers and teams. Many of us don't get to the 'acceptance of rejection' stage. We get stuck in the phase of anger, despair and dejection.

Unfortunately, this attribution bias protects our self-esteem, but prevents us from learning from the rejection. This is all the more true when you have cleared the IAS exam, I suppose.

In contrast, those who are able to make a comeback from a career setback take a different route to salvation. Instead of getting stuck in the grief stage, they actively explore what went wrong, and if they were to be blamed for the fiasco. They also try and figure out how they could have done it differently, if they get a second chance. And most importantly, they actively seek feedback from a wide set of people, including peers, superiors and even subordinates. They insist that they want transparent feedback not some words of consolation.

In the story we saw earlier the IAS officer who had been sent to head a PSU had a vibrant network in Delhi and when alerted he decided to take quick action before the proverbial ink had dried on his extension letter. Taking that action at that time saved the day.

Think back about a situation when you went through a career setback—say, a job you wanted was not given to you. The company decided to hire someone from outside at a fancy package. How did you react to this setback? Did you curse and cry to your colleagues? Did you start cursing your company and the boss? Did you start applying for a job outside the moment the announcement was made? Did you spread gloom and doom all around your office?

Or did you politely ask for time from your boss and maybe his boss? And when you got the time, did you seek their views on why the company did not consider you, but went outside for the much-desired new role?

Seeking an audience and getting their views is a way to get to a better place. Maybe, you found out that they thought very highly of you and were in fact thinking of saving you for a better assignment. Or they thought you were good, but had some issues in dealing with your peers. Now that was a good learning outcome. You could have sought to find out how you could get better in dealing with your peers. You could request your superior or someone from a related team to become your mentor, so that they could guide you in your development journey.

Career setbacks and rejection are common both in government jobs and in the private sector. Unlike in the private sector the type of rejections that are handed out to you in government service are more complex and could be shrouded in secrecy. But if you have a vibrant rejection processing system, you can decode the rejection and figure out your next course of action.

Reframing a rejection as an opportunity to learn is true both in government service and in private sector

It calls for some serious soul-searching. Your career can get derailed if you escape from your current reality and rejection, by seeking refuge in obfuscation and rumour-mongering. But if you can stop getting derailed, stay on track, learn from the rejection and setback, you could avoid getting destroyed and instead become stronger and better. The rules apply even more if you are in government service. The choice is yours.

> **TAKEAWAY:** *Whichever sector you work in, remember rejection is a part of the long journey of life. Don't let a rejection or two derail you. Learn to use your internal spring to face the rejection and bounce forward.*

Embracing and Learning from Rejection

One who gains strength by overcoming obstacles possesses the only strength which can overcome adversity.

—Albert Schweitzer

Prof. Ranjan Banerjee, dean of S.P. Jain Institute of Management and Research (SPJIMR) tells an amusing story about how an acquaintance of his, a PhD research fellow in the US, so dreaded the (rejection) mail from a reputed publication that he did not open the mail for four months. Yes, for full four months the mail was lying unopened in his inbox. He would see it every day, but would not open the mail knowing fully well that it was a rejection. Finally, a colleague had to nudge him hard to open the mail which was indeed a 'rejection'. Fortunately, it was not the end of the road for him. The rejection set him off on a path that got him to rework that paper and get it published a few months later.

Academics the world over have a love-hate relationship with the word 'rejection'. In the international world of academics, irrespective of your name and status, your paper can get rejected by a peer-reviewed journal. Or your research proposal can get rejected by the foundation to which you have applied for funding. And worse still, you may face rejection in the class room. The system prepares you to face the first two types of rejection. Unfortunately, rejection in the classroom is more common in India, sometimes very public and career-destroying. So a young faculty can go through a harrowing time, especially if they are not prepared and don't have a good support system to fall back on.

Prof. Banerjee says very emphatically that rejection was not the issue, because success would follow failure and rejection. And good academics know that rejection is a stepping stone to success. He himself went to the US to pursue his PhD at the age of thirty-eight and had his own share of rejections till he figured out what he needed to do to get accepted. He makes a strong point when he says that: '*Ability to take failure or rejection and handling it well is the single biggest differentiator for success.*'

Academics who enjoy the research process take these adverse outcomes as a part of the learning process. A balance of success and rejection in fact helps in building self-esteem. Good academics are not outcome-focused but are learning-obsessed. And a good PhD scholar knows that it is in fact an entrepreneurial journey. You need to view each disappointment and rejection as an opportunity to learn.

Staci Zavattaro—Six Steps

1. Put it away
2. Everyone gets rejected
3. Speaking of thick skin
4. See rejection as a learning opportunity
5. Ask for help
6. Have fun

Staci Zavattaro in the *LSE Impact Blog* (9 April 2019) writing about academic rejection says that there are six steps to handling rejection in academic life:

- **Put it away**—Rejection often hits hard. So put the reviews away and look at them after you have created sufficient mind space to handle them.

- **Everyone gets rejected**—Don't think for a moment just because you are a 'small name' you are facing more rejection. It is a blind process and even the biggest names get rejected. Often. So you better develop a thick skin.

- **Speaking of a thick skin**—You really do need one. Rejection should bother you but it cannot affect you. You cannot get devastated by a rejection.

- **See rejection as a learning opportunity**—From each rejection comes a silver lining—if you let it.

- **Ask for help**—Do not be afraid to ask others for feedback or input. Talk to friends. All I am suggesting is that you do not hold in rejection, because perhaps from talking comes a partnership you did not expect, or an idea you never would have had previously.

- **Have fun**—Sometimes in academia we like to have a 'busy competition.' It is where everyone tries to out-busy the other. People compare projects they worked on during spring break. Instead, go have fun. Clear your mind. Do something you love. Really, it does not matter what. Just do it. Your work will be there when you get back.

Prof. Ratti Rathneshwar of University of Missouri, while addressing a seminar on academic publishing at SPJIMR, reiterated many of the points made above. He also presented two ways of responding to a rejection. The first was what he called the '**disaster sequence**' and it consisted of anger, denial, disregard and even counter-attack. The more productive response is what he calls the '**success sequence**' and here one studied the rejection, didn't rush with the response and let cool cognition overcome hot emotion (shades of '**fixed mindset**' and '**growth mindset**' we saw earlier).

Venki Ramakrishnan, who won the Nobel Prize in Chemistry in 2009, had been given many indications that he would not win the big prize. As he recounts in his book *Gene Machine*, Jim Watson '… peered at me intently with his bulging eyes and said my work was beautiful but really I shouldn't worry about Stockholm because not getting the prize was not the end of the world.' To clarify, it was Jim Watson with Francis Crick who cracked the double helix structure of the human DNA and had won the Nobel Prize in Physiology or Medicine in 1962. And the Stockholm he was referring to was the Nobel Award Organisation which was headquartered in Stockholm, Sweden. But Venki Ramakrishnan did win the Nobel Prize just a few years after his run-in with Jim Watson.

What can you learn from these academics?

For one there is the whole process known as 'peer review'. Every respectable journal has a peer-review process. The same is true of the more coveted conferences and awards. What you submit is often sent to two or more experts for their comments. They opine if the paper can be 'accepted' or 'rejected' or 'accepted subject to changes'. The real work begins after getting the peer review feedback. Academics who do the peer review take their job very seriously. And those who get the review/feedback look forward to the peer-review report. The names are hidden on both sides so that there is no bias. Can the system be gamed? Maybe, but we will not go there. Most respected academics understand the importance of the peer review process. A paper submitted to a journal may undergo several revisions and that could take a year or more.

The process of getting your research published and accepted by the fellow research community is an agonising one filled with rejection. Some of the starters never get past the first hurdle. But those that do figure out that rejection is nothing but a feedback loop, start enjoying the rejection, almost. They figure out that they can use each rejection as an opportunity to become better.

The peer review process is so thorough that even the most respected of academics can get their papers rejected. A bit like Albert Einstein getting a rejection email from the *Journal of Relativity*. It may have happened.

Those in corporate sector would find this to be rather quaint. How can you get rejected time and again, yet continue to do your research? Are these academics human at all?

The world of academia lives and breathes a different rejection mantra. They see rejection not as a dead-end street but as a pointer to what can be done better. As I said, a rejection mail often contains very valuable tips of how you need to change your research project to make it better.

Let us play this out in the corporate sector.

You are standing up and presenting your new idea to your bosses. In the room are also many of your colleagues, or peers. After you present, they give you their feedback and your proposal is rejected. Now if it was in an academic setting, you will also get inputs on how you need to rework your proposal (assuming that it had some gem of an idea worth saving). And you can get a chance to represent it to a different panel the coming month or year.

Can we see rejection differently? Can we see it as a way to improve ourselves?

Play it differently. How boring our life would be if we never got rejected. If we never got rejected, it may in fact mean that we are playing in a small field. We are not taking chances outside our comfort zone. That could in itself be a self-limiting belief.

I have had subordinates walking up to me saying, 'I don't know why I should report to this guy. He says yes to anything I propose. Is he not supposed to give me critical feedback?' This has led to counselling sessions with those superiors who had to be told that your job is not to win the popularity contest. At times I have had to temper my feedback only to get a knowing smirk from my team saying, 'You are not your natural self,

Ambi. Why don't you let it rip? Don't hold back, we want to know what you really think about this idea.'

A Johns Hopkins University study from the *Journal of Experimental Psychology* points towards an interesting phenomenon: *rejection can inspire more imaginative thinking.* The study involved students with one group being given a 'rejected by friends' message and told to solve a set of problems. The control group was not given a rejected message. The research found that students exhibiting a more independent self-concept showed greater creativity after being rejected. When hiring, we are biased towards people who have never been rejected, says Prof. Sharon Kim, but people who have handled rejection may actually have a lot to offer as an individual contributor, than a so-called super-star candidate. Again, maybe we should ask for a rejection résumé along with the normal résumé.

So should you start loving rejection? Should you seek rejection?

Getting ready to face rejection means you are stretching your limits of performance. You know that you are trying to go somewhere where you may never have ventured before. You are proposing something that may appear risky at first. You are probably making some bold assumptions as you make your pitch to your bosses. You may have all the back-up reasons for arguing your case. But will they be accepted?

Why Seek Rejection—Robert D. Smith

1. Makes you fearless
2. Makes you do something
3. Strengthens all parts of your life
4. Makes you motivated
5. Leads to a more fulfilling life

In his article 'Seek Rejection', Robert D. Smith says that there are clearly five reasons you should seek rejection. Firstly, seeking rejection makes you fearless. You are ready to face 'No' as many as thirty or forty times a day in your sales job or from your venture capital investor. Can you train yourself to feel happy when you get a rejection? Or at least not feel distraught?

Secondly, seeking rejection forces you to do something. It takes fear out of the equation, it becomes easier to take action and not procrastinate. Imagine the situation of a person who waited a week to respond to a mail. Or took months to open a mail fearing that it was a rejection as we saw in the first part of this chapter.

Thirdly, seeking rejection will strengthen all parts of your life. It is impossible to be fearless in only your work life. Your sense of fearlessness will creep into other parts of your life. You will become a fearless friend, ready to help others. You will become a fearless spouse, encouraging your partner to boldly venture forth, casting aside fears of rejection. You will be a fearless parent, helping your children fly high.

Fourthly, as you seek rejection, you will feel massively motivated. Imagine facing multiple rejections yet accepting it with a smile. Nothing will demotivate you anymore. You are hyper-charged all the time. Finally, he says that as you seek rejection you will end up becoming rich, both monetarily and in life.

Steve Jobs was rejected by the Apple board at one point. He went out there to found Pixar Studios that redefined animation movies; and he went back to Apple to make it the shining star of the digital world. Michael Jordan was rejected from his eighth-grade basketball team, and he ended up winning six NBA titles.

Colonel Sanders, the founder of Kentucky Fried Chicken (KFC), was fired from several businesses before he started his chicken business. He was a full forty-years-old when he started cooking chicken at his Shell Service Station in 1930. He took more than a decade to perfect his secret recipe, and faced setbacks during the Great Depression and World War II. Finally, his chicken became popular, not before it had been rejected more than a thousand times by potential partners. Failure and rejections never defeated Colonel Sanders. KFC is today the second largest fast food restaurant chain in the world. Colonel Sanders famously said, '*One has to remember that every failure can be a stepping stone to something better.*'

There is always a positive side to a failure or rejection.

Steward Butterfield was trying to design a videogame when he realised that his dream project was not working out. He instead used certain features from this to start a successful photo-sharing platform, Flickr which was sold to Yahoo a few years later for a hefty $25 million. In the meantime, Butterfield was working on yet another videogame called Glitch. This too failed when it was launched. But Butterfield was unfazed, he rebranded a feature from the failed Glitch into an in-house platform for employees to communicate with each other, at work. That led to the immensely successful chat service called Slack. So a rejection, a failure can teach you new lessons and new ideas you never thought you had in the first place.

As Yuval Noah Harari points out in his book *21 Lessons for the 21st Century*, to discover new ideas you have to be ready to give space and accept rejection: 'Yet if you want to go deeply into any subject, you need a lot of time, and in particular you need the privilege of wasting time. You need to experiment with unproductive paths, to explore dead ends, to make space for doubts and boredom, and to allow little seeds of insight to slowly grow and blossom. If you cannot afford to waste time— you will never find the truth.' If I may add, if you cannot accept rejection with a smile, you will end up not finding anything.

You probably think that it is easy for me to say that you should seek rejection and not be scared of it. You may laugh at this advice. But think back. Getting accepted and not getting rejected is not in your hands. Whether you like it or not, you may get rejected. You have two options facing you. You can try and do things that will never get rejected. And that will restrict your span of activities and make for a monotonous life which you will get pretty tired of.

The other option is to try things that may, or should I say will get rejected. You should try and make those rather outlandish proposals that will get rejected. My friend, innovation coach R. Sridhar says that in his workshops the one question he puts to the participants is: 'What is the one idea that you have that will surely get rejected by the powers that be?' And that leads to an interesting discussion on why it will get rejected.

You should try and do things that will get rejected. Now comes the second subroutine. What do you do when you get rejected? You can take the rejection to heart and feel devastated.

The other option is to embrace the rejection. Instead of reacting negatively, you process the rejection in stages. Feel bad for a bit. But then start finding out what happened, and why you got rejected. As you learn more, you can pivot the rejection into a learning exercise. You will be able to turn a rejected proposal around into something even bigger and grander.

Just as we say with the academicians, we can all learn to react to rejection differently. And more importantly we can all learn to embrace rejection with a lot of gusto. A rejection today could indeed be a stepping stone to a bigger success tomorrow. Just as a polite nod today may end up becoming a missed opportunity tomorrow.

In her book, *Resilience* Liggy Webb, an international speaker on life skills, has an interesting term for reframing a problem into an opportunity. She calls it 'probortunities'. She says you can be positive and view your problems as opportunities. Identify and understand each problem, be creative and explore a range of options, learn and get better at taking decisions. I think you can look at each rejection with the opportunity window and so reframe a rejection into a 'rejbortunity'. A rejection that can open up a new window, a new opportunity.

Best-selling author Jeff Keller in his book *The Winning Attitude* presents yet another way of working with rejections. He says you have the choice to view your difficulties as opportunities, learning experiences and challenges for growth. You need to rewire your brain, accept the emotions, ask others for examples on how negative situations in their life turned out to be positives and most importantly, take an inventory of your rejections and see how they could have been turned positive.

You can see rejection as the end game. OR, you can see rejection as a need to 'review'.

If you can see each rejection as a need to review, you too will start loving rejections. Your job application got rejected. You need to review what you write in your CV. You got rejected at the interview stage. What did you say? How did you answer the questions? You need to review your interview strategy. You join the company but got rejected when you asked to be posted in a particular division or unit. What happened? Can you review the situation? Did you make a wrong request? Or did you make it at the wrong time? Don't worry about the rejection. See it as a 'need to review'.

Learn to love rejection. Understand that it can help you become better. Get the fear of rejection out of your system. And you will continue to spring upwards and onwards.

TAKEAWAY: *Realise that a rejection often holds some valuable lessons for you to rise higher. Learn to embrace rejection and not live in fear of them. And get every rejection to make you become a little bit better.*

Resilience—The Spring Mechanism

A good half of the art of living is resilience.

—Alain de Botton

The prognosis was not good. Ashok (name changed) was told that even with chemotherapy he might not make it beyond a few months. Everyone around him was shocked. His family. His friends. His colleagues. People were wondering if he would be willing to meet them. Was it even allowed when you were going through an intense chemo, they wondered.

An old friend wanted to meet him and decided to call Ashok and ask if he was free to meet him and a few other old friends from his professional life. What he heard as a reply was a big surprise: 'I am more than happy to meet old friends. So please come home and let us have an enjoyable evening together. But on one condition—you or the other two scoundrels you will bring along are not permitted to ask me anything about my illness. Is that understood?'

The three old warriors landed up at Ashok's home soon after. What was to be a short 'Hello, how are you' meeting ended up lasting more than four hours, with endless drinks, samosas, kebabs and more. They spent four hours laughing about old stories, gossiping about industry foibles and the future trends. It was a riotous four hours, not something you would expect to spend with someone who probably had just a few months left to live. As they left his house, or should I say staggered out of his house, they were left wondering, 'Is this guy really sick?' What was happening here? By the way, eventually the chemo worked and Ashok managed to defeat the big C, hands down.

How can someone who had just a few months to live cheer up people who had called on him to cheer him up?

Imagine this. You are locked away in a death camp. You see people dying around you every day. Even children, women and elderly are not spared from the death chambers. How do you stay alive? How do you keep your spirit alive? Do you think about tomorrow, next week, next month? Or something more.

In his book, *Man's Search For Meaning*, Viktor Frankl describes his days at the Nazi concentration camp and how he managed to stay alive. As he says, 'We must never forget that we may also find meaning in life even when confronted with a hopeless situation, when facing a fate that cannot be changed.' He managed to live because he stopped thinking about getting that next cigarette, or that last bowl of soup. Instead, he focused on something in the distant future. He started imagining that one day in the future after the war was over he would be giving a lecture to a rapt audience about the psychology of the concentration camp in order to help others understand what he went through. Was he sure that he would come out alive from the ordeal? No, definitely not.

But by focusing on a long-term goal he was able to rise well above the suffering of the moment

Researchers who studied the experiences of soldiers who survived long periods of incarceration in POW camps have found a strange truth. The soldiers who imagined their world in the long-term, maybe a few years ahead, managed to survive and come out in one piece. Those soldiers who were counting days and weeks ended up becoming mental wrecks, if they survived the period in captivity at all.

Frankl's theory and his book is possibly one of the first expositions of what is today a hot topic in business coaching: *resilence training*. It is simply a way of getting people to construct more meaning in their everyday life.

What is resilience?

Resilience comes from the Latin word 'resalire' which means springing back.

Al Siebert in his book *The Resiliency Advantage* has defined resilience in vivid terms. He says it is the ability to cope well with high levels of ongoing disruptive change, sustain good health and energy when under pressure, bounce back easily from setbacks and overcome adversities. It is also the ability to change to a new way of working and living, when an old one is no longer possible. It is to do all this without getting dysfunctional or harmful. Siebert points out that 'resile' is a verb, so it is something that you 'do' rather than something that you 'have'.

Karen Reivich and Andrew Shatte in their book *The Resilience Factor* say that 'resilience is the ability to bounce back from setbacks, learn from failure, be motivated by challenges and believe in your own abilities to deal with the stress and difficulties of life'.

Jeffrey Davis in his *Psychology Today* article defines resilience in a more simple way:

'It is your ability to face down rejection and criticism on your way to success.'

Criticism and rejection should be seen not as something that will weaken us, but as thing that will make us stronger and in fact help us embolden our creative ideas and output.

Each of us have a different way, a different algorithm to handle rejection and failure. Matin Seligman, the guru of positive psychology says, 'Failure is one of life's most common traumas, yet people's responses to it vary widely. Some bounce back (or bounce forward as we saw earlier in this book), after a brief period of malaise; others descend into depression and a paralysing fear of the future.'

Your career hit a plateau. You managed to join a struggling MNC as its head of sales but knew that you will have to bail out soon. One of the most respected global corporations call you for a job. You manage to land the job. You join and then discover that the company has had a change of heart. You are given a much smaller assignment than what had been indicated during the interview stage. Should you get dejected or should you carry on as if this is the most important job on earth? Well, I know of someone who showed his resilience by bouncing back full of energy in that small assignment. Only to find that his career take off like a rocket.

That is resilience.

How do *you* become resilient?

Children are resilient. They are by nature curious, playful and willing to go where they have never gone before.

Diane L. Coutu in her article 'How Resilience Works' (*Harvard Business Review*, May 2002) says resilient people possess three key defining characteristics. They coolly accept the harsh realities facing them. Instead of slipping into a denial mood, they take a sober down-to-earth view of the reality of the situation. They then find meaning in terrible times. (See how Viktor Frankl's words keep coming back when we delve deeper into resilience training). They don't lament saying 'why me', but they devise constructs about the suffering and manage to build mental bridges from the present day funk to a much better future. These mental bridges make the present situation more manageable. Finally, they are able to creatively improvise. They are able to make do with what they have. They put resources together, explore unfamiliar uses and imagine possibilities.

Diane L. Coutu—Three Characteristics of Resilient People

1. Accept the harsh reality facing you
2. Find meaning in terrible times
3. Creatively improvise

Sriram was a passionate marketing executive. He had done his MBA from one of the better B-Schools in Mumbai. He started his career with an Indian healthcare company and managed to navigate the troubled waters of a typical family-managed

Indian company. But he soon realised that he was not learning enough. He took the risk to move to a lower-level sales manager role in an MNC. But he found his immediate boss obnoxious. He moved to another MNC only to discover that his obnoxious boss had followed him to his new company. What was he to do? His resilience muscle showed up. He decided to venture out into the world of marketing communication in healthcare, and soon landed an even better job. If he had stayed back and moped around, wonder where he would have landed up.

What would you have done if you were in this situation?

There are ways you can become more resilient. You can change the way you think, change the way you act, change the way you communicate. Put together these and it will make a big difference to your own resiliency factor.

So is being resilient just about being positive irrespective of what is happening around you?

Doug Hench in his book *Positively Resilient* says that there are several myths around who we think are resilient.

- Resilient people are really positive and upbeat almost all the time. Not true—the really resilient people may be a little bit more positive in their outlook but they reserve the option of calling upon the most effective emotion in the moment.
- Resilient people are known for being able to go through it alone without the help of others. Not true—every successful resilient person had strong

connections with a host of people who facilitated their success and their resilience.

- Resilient people are the ones who never give up. Not true—resilient people do make a realistic assessment of their chances, while being optimistic. And they are adept at making the right switch at the most opportune time.

- Resilient people take so much pride in what they do that they tend to be perfectionists. Not true—in reality, it is good to be proud of what you do but expecting not to make any mistakes, to succeed in everything you do, is just setting yourself up for disappointment and dejection.

Martin Seligman in his book *Learned Optimism* points towards a few traits of successful people. They are physically healthier, less likely to suffer from depression, more likely to do well in school, more productive at work and more likely to win in sports. Now not all of us are good at all this. But you get the picture. An optimistic person reacts to the same situation differently from a person not so optimistic. When an optimistic person gets diagnosed with a heart condition, he takes it upon himself to fix his lifestyle, his diet and his sleeping habits. The pessimistic thinker may say, the heart condition runs in my family, I can't do much. You can see how an optimistic person internalised the issue and decided to fix it. On the other hand, the pessimistic person quickly externalised the issue and disowned the problem.

We can all become more resilient if we can look at rejection and failure not as the end of the road but as a speed breaker

The good news is that your system is not hardwired with a level of resilience. You can become more and more resilient as you get older and you develop some good habits like mindfulness meditation.

How can we improve our own resilience quotient? Are there some tools? In the book *Resilience*, Andrew Zolli and Mary Ann Healy point towards the power of mindfulness meditation. They ask a question, 'Can meditation serve as a resilience booster, inoculating the brain against anxiety and stress and, possibly genetic influences like the variant of the 5-HTT gene?'

The 5-HTT gene or at least the shorter variant of the gene has been shown to render subjects more vulnerable to adversity. In an effort to answer their question they point to research that seems to confirm that subjects who meditated were found to have dramatically increased their sense of mindfulness (being able to observe one's experience in a nonreactive manner), purpose in life (viewing one's life as meaningful, worthwhile and aligned with long term goals and values), and decreased neuroticism (negative emotionality).

Sudha (name changed) was a super star performer in this marketing services firm. She managed some key accounts and also did a stellar job in a planning role. But she was keen on exploring the big world of marketing. She was keen on working in an FMCG company in a marketing role. She knew it was difficult to move after more than a decade-and-a-half in marketing services to a true-blue marketing company. But she tried and managed to land a job as marketing manager in an Indian FMCG company. While her former colleagues warned her of the problems she would face, she was ill-prepared for what was to come twelve months later. One fine day she went to office and saw a notice posted on the door. The MD of the company, also the owner of the company, had written a letter to all the employees of the company that he has sold the company to a big Indian firm. And each of the employees would be given possible opportunities in the new merged entity. Sudha was shell-shocked since just a few days prior to this notice a newspaper had speculated on these lines and she had been promised by her immediate boss that 'nothing was happening'. Though she could have gone back to the world of marketing services, she decided to look for opportunities in marketing and as luck would have it managed to land an even better job. And this led to better positions in marketing and more. She demonstrated tremendous resilience when faced with a shocking incident. And over the years, she has managed to become more resilient.

To be resilient you need to be ready to accept reality the way it is, and not end up blaming someone else for your problems, your rejection

You then need to have a strong deep belief in what you do, your values, your meaning in life. And finally, you need to be able to improvise in any situation. Even if you have one of these qualities, you can bounce back from a rejection. But if you have all three in abundant measure you can be truly resilient. And as you become resilient, every rejection, every failure, makes you so much more stronger and better.

Claude Levi-Strauss is possibly one of the most famous anthropologists ever. He pioneered studies to understand the lives of Amazonian Indians. He used the term 'skill bricolage' to describe the way we bounce back from obstacles. Etymologically speaking the word 'bricolage' comes from the French 'bricoler' which means 'to tinker'. Levi Strauss says, 'In its old sense, the verb bricolage … was always used with reference to some extraneous movement: a ball rebounding, a dog straying, or a horse swerving from its direct course to avoid an obstacle.' We can form a modern point of view and say that bricolage is inventiveness and the ability to improvise a solution without proper material or tools. So resilient people are good at bricolage; they are ready to tinker around and make the most of what they have. In a concentration camp, the resourceful resilient inmates knew to pocket pieces of string, knowing that they would become useful for something—keep a shirt together or a shoe from falling apart.

If you are in a corporate role, you have to be aware that rejection is going to happen. But what does it do to you? Do you feel dejected? Let down? Defeated? Or do you see it as a part of reality and draw on your inner meaning? Are you able to bricolage a possible solution to get you to a better place?

Steven Spielberg was rejected three times from film school before he was accepted. Oprah Winfrey was fired from her first job as a TV anchor. Harrison Ford was told after his first 'two-line' role that he was never going to make it in the movie business.

And see how they managed to rise above these rejections.

Remember Viktor Frankl's words as you face rejection, 'Everything can be taken from a man but one thing—the last of human freedoms—to choose one's attitude in any given circumstances, to choose one's own way.'

Choose your way carefully and be ready to spring back after any rejection.

> **TAKEAWAY:** *Remember the opposite of rejection is not ebullience, but resilience. Discover your own internal resilience spring. And you will always spring back after any rejection.*

Summing Up: SPRING Back. SPRING Forward.

Never give up. Today is hard. Tomorrow will be worse,
but the day after tomorrow will be sunshine.

—Jack Ma

Congratulations! If you have reached this far in the book you have managed to climb *the three peaks of rejection management.* The first peak is about anticipating and facing rejection, the second peak is about processing and recovering from rejection and the final peak is learning and progressing after rejection.

If we can understand and master the art of climbing the three peaks, no rejection is going to upset our plans.

But why does managing rejection matter?

There is this old parable attributed to Gautama Buddha. A woman, whose young child had passed away and was grief-stricken approached Buddha weeping, begging him to heal her from her suffering. The Buddha told her that he could help her but before he does that he wanted her to visit each and every house in her village and collect a mustard seed from each house that has not had a bereavement. The woman set out in all earnest to collect the mustard seeds, with the hope that her suffering would soon be over. But she returned to the Buddha a few days later with no mustard seeds since she found that every house she visited had experienced a death in the family, in the not-too-distant past. She realised that what she was going through was not uncommon. She was not being singled out to suffer intense emotional pain. She was not alone.

Now we can replay the same story by replacing bereavement with rejection. To put it simply, rejection is universal.

In this book, we have looked at rejection through various filters. I have shared many stories from my campus days to my days in marketing and my long innings in advertising. We have also read about how business leaders, authors, athletes, sports persons, world champions, senior bureaucrats, academicians of repute, space scientists, Nobel laureates, movie directors, much-lauded musicians, start-up entrepreneurs and more have faced rejection. Clearly, everyone has faced rejection. The successful ones have faced rejection many times. And conquered the rejections.

Here are three interesting views on rejection and failure.

Thomas J Watson, the founder of the global corporation IBM had this to say: 'Success is on the far side of failure.'

The genius scientist Albert Einstein said, 'In the middle of difficulty lies opportunity.'

And the wonderful British actress Emma Thomson says this about failure, 'My dad once said to me, if you can't fail you can't do anything, and it was brilliant advice. That made me see that it's important not to be afraid.'

To be successful you should be ready to face rejection and failure

If you have mastered the three-stage rejection handling programme I have presented, no rejection is going to set you back. You will be able to bounce forward with every rejection.

Why is handling rejection going to be more and more important in the years ahead?

We are entering an interesting phase in the growth of our country. Opportunities are going to be everywhere. And now is the time for you to take that step outside your comfort zone. You may not succeed the first time. But if you don't venture out you are going to be like a deer stunned by the headlight of an oncoming car, caught in the middle of the road wondering whether to go back or go forward.

What opportunities am I talking about?

When I was the president of the Advertising Club of Bombay [now Mumbai] we celebrated the fiftieth anniversary of the club. To mark the occasion we had a day-long celebration of events, workshops, seminars etc. We also got the veteran journalist and business strategist Anita Sharan to create a handy book entitled *50 Careers in Advertising.* This was in 2004.

If the club were to create a new book of advertising careers in the 2020s, it would probably have 200 career options to list out. The relatively small world of advertising has exploded with opportunities. Imagine other sectors like finance, healthcare, supply-chain, travel/tourism, human resources, information technology, media/entertainment etc.

For a person who is in the age group of twenty-five to forty there are innumerable opportunities, whichever sector you choose to enter. These opportunities come in many forms. There are career opportunities and there are entrepreneurial opportunities. And I am seeing a number of highly qualified youngsters kicking up a well-paying job to get on the entrepreneurial road, knowing fully well that the road is going to be filled with potholes called rejection.

There are people and some experts who also present a gloomy picture about how technology will take over all our jobs and all of us will become redundant in a few years. I suppose the same fears were expressed when electricity was becoming affordable. Ditto for the internet.

Even in India when Prime Minister Narasimha Rao decided to reduce the taxes (excise duties as they were known) on washing machines from 65 per cent to 15 per cent, a leftist politician is said to have protested saying, 'What will all those poor women who get employment as housemaids do now that you have made washing machines so affordable?' To this, the inscrutable PM is reported to have replied, 'Do you want our women to stay as maids all their lives?'

Young readers may not know how violently bank employees of state-run banks protested computerisation, fearing loss of jobs.

Any technology wave—be it steam power or electricity or computerisation or the internet—will cause disruption in the way we work and live. An *Economist* article (29 June 2019) says that 47 per cent of American jobs are at high risk of automation by the mid-2030s. This could spell doomsday. But it could also mean that so many newer jobs are going to be opening up for the young to grab.

As Ajit Balakrishnan, founder of Rediff.com says in his article in the *Business Standard* (4 March 2020), 'It is probably an urgent necessity that machine learning algorithm skills be made part of the curricula in medical colleges, law schools, engineering disciplines as well as for undergraduate courses even in commerce and humanities. *This will enable young Indians to step forward into the emerging world with confidence* (italics mine).'

I remember when I introduced the concept of a computerised spreadsheet (using an IBM PC) in Boots Company in the year 1995, I was pooh-poohed. The company had a computer centre in its Sion office and you had to take off your shoes before you entered it (look how we equated a computer centre to a holy place). How can a small computer do the work in just one day? I did have a few anxious moments but the experiment of developing month-wise, district-wise, sales budgets for the entire sales team of 250 in just one day worked. And in a few months, the idea of using a PC for such mundane calculations became the norm. More than twenty-five clerical staff got trained on basic spreadsheet skills. And many of them mastered the skill pretty fast. Not a single person lost his or her job.

What has all this got to do with facing rejection?

If you have a rejection processing mechanism hardwired into your brain, you will be able to grab all the exciting new opportunities that are going to be available for you. If however you continue to be scared of rejection and failure, you are going to end up becoming redundant soon.

Not all of us handle rejection the same way. In fact, culturally each of us are hardwired differently. The Japanese consider rejection and failure to be terminal, though there is this fabulous Japanese proverb, 'Nara korobi ya oki' (fall seven times, rise eight). In America, failure is something that is part and parcel of getting better. In India, I think we used to see rejection and failure as a permanent 'black mark'. So youngsters were scared of setting up their own ventures. A safe government job or a job with a respected industrial group was seen as a lot better than setting out on your own. A job in a rather risky business like advertising (or media or marketing services) was also looked down upon, as I can say from my own experience.

Fortunately, that is changing and I see this from the CVs of talented youngsters who are being recruited by my current client companies. A failure in a start-up venture is not seen as a bad thing at all. In many cases it is seen as an added bonus.

Michelle Obama tells us how a college counsellor told her 'I'm not sure that you're Princeton material', giving her a perfunctory patronising smile, if you please. This did not change Michelle Obama's desire to get into Princeton. And she recounts in her book, *Becoming*, 'I wasn't going to let one person's opinion dislodge everything I thought I knew about myself... I switched my method without changing my goal. I would apply to Princeton and a scattershot selection of other schools, but without any more input from the college counsellor. Instead, I sought help from someone who actually knew me. Mr. Smith, my assistant principal and neighbour, had seen my strengths as a student and furthermore trusted me with his own kids.'

Michelle Obama had her rejection processing system that helped her navigate a rejection well. Do you have one ready?

In the previous chapters, we looked at various aspects of how people handle the rejections they have been handed out. While you will develop your own method, which you should, let us review the simple three-step process outlined for handling rejection.

The first stage of handling rejection is the ability to anticipate and accept rejection. Don't take it personally. Quieten your inner critic.

The second stage is processing and recovering from rejection. Can you decode the rejection message? Is it a hard rejection or a soft one? Who can you go to for support? Do you have a confidant who can help you?

The third and final stage is learning and progressing after rejection. What can you learn from the rejection? What mistake did you make and should avoid making the next time? What lesson did you learn?

Three Stage Handling of Rejection

1. Anticipating and Accepting Rejection
2. Processing and Recovering from Rejection
3. Learning and Progressing after Rejection

Pema Chodron, the much-loved American Tibetan Buddhist teacher in her book *Fail, Fail Again, Fail Better* says that failing better means that when these things (failures/rejections) happen in your life they become a source of growth, a source of forward, a source of out-of-that-place rawness with which you can really communicate genuinely with other people.

Failing better means that failure becomes a rich and fertile ground (for learning) instead of just another slap in the face

Nelson Mandela had said, 'Do not judge me by my successes; judge me by how many times I fell down and got back up again.' As someone who spent twenty-seven years in prison only to come out and lead his country towards full democracy and freedom, knows only too well that great successes are built on the foundations of great failures and rejections.

Ikigai is the Japanese secret to a long and happy life. In their eponymous book, Hector Garcia and Francesc Miralles say that the secret of long life is ikigai, which in Japanese means 'the happiness of always being busy'. How do we find our own ikigai, in spite of all the hurdles, failures and rejections we may face?

All of us have it in us to be successful. One ingredient is our ability to manage rejection and failure. You could call it 'resilience' or 'grit'.

In their article in _Harvard Business Review_ (September—October 2018), Prof. Thomas H Lee and Prof. Angela Duckworth have this to say about grit: 'High achievers have extraordinary stamina. Even if they're already at the top of their game, they're always striving to improve. Even if their work requires sacrifice, they remain in love with what they do. Even when easier paths beckon, their commitment is steadfast. We call this remarkable combination of strengths "grit". Grit predicts who will accomplish challenging goals. Research done at West Point (USA's military training academy), for example, shows that it's a better indicator of which cadets will make it through training than achievement test scores and athletic ability. Grit predicts the likelihood of graduating from high school and college and performance in stressful jobs such as sales. Grit, also we believe, propels people to the highest ranks of leadership in many demanding fields.'

I do hope the book you have in your hand has given you some tips on how to manage rejection, develop resilience and grit, so that you can always be busy and always be happy.

There is always the *Serenity Prayer* by Reinhold Niebuhr to fall back on:

> God, grant me the Serenity
> To accept the things I cannot change …
> Courage to change the things I can,
> And Wisdom to know the difference.

And from the *Bhagavad Gita* we find a stanza that was probably written a couple of millennia ago that captures the spirit of doing your duty, without waiting for the fruits of your labour:

> *karmany evaadhikaaraste*
> *maa phaleshu kadaachana*
> *maa karma phala hetur bhoor*
> *maa te sango' stvakarmani*

'You have a right is to perform your prescribed duty, but you are not entitled to the fruits of your action. Never consider yourself the cause of the results of your activities, and never be attached to not doing your duty'.

With those words Lord Krishna motivated Arjuna to perform his duty. Irrespective of the fear of failure or rejection.

Writing this book, speaking with so many people, reading all those wonderful books and articles has been a great learning journey for me. I do hope my words on facing rejection and powering ahead have instilled in you a new booster dose of self-confidence and courage to go boldly ahead, face rejection, embrace it, learn from it and progress further in your chosen career, business, artistic field or profession.

May you SPRING back after every rejection you face,
achieve what you set out to achieve and live
a happy successful life.

TAKEAWAY: *Be focused about what you do, but be ready to face rejection. Have a rejection processing system and use it to learn from every rejection. Develop your internal system, be ready to face any rejection and spring back.*

SPRING BACK by Handling Rejections Better

Seven Worksheets

#1 Rejection Recall (Rejection Résumé)

List the many small and big rejections you have faced in your life. These could be work related, education/student life related or relationship related. Put down the top four, that you remember. These may have had the maximum impact on your life.

1. ......

2. ......

3. ......

4. ......

#2 First Reaction

Think back. What was your first reaction to the rejection? Were you even remotely prepared to hear the rejection? Or was it a total surprise? How did you react to the rejection when you got it? Did the rejection lead to a long period of dejection? Or did you bounce back immediately?

From what you have learnt from this book, what will be your reaction if you got the same rejection today? How will your 'first reaction' be different?

Rejection First	Reaction Then	First Reaction Now
1.		
2.		
3.		
4.		

#3 After Rejection Response

What was your reaction one day later, one week later, one month later? Was it different from what it was when you got the rejection?

From what you have learnt from the book, what will be your new post-facto reaction to rejection? How will it be different from how you reacted post-facto the first time?

Rejection	*Post-Facto Then*	*Post-Facto Now*
1.		
2.		
3.		
4.		

#4 What is your Support System?

Who did you share your rejection news with when it happened? What was their feedback? How did it help you?

What will be the support group if the rejection were to happen today? How do you think it will be better?

Who is your support group today—friends, family, mentors, colleagues? Do you have a list of four people to go to?

Rejection	*Support System Then*	*Support System Now*
1.		
2.		
3.		
4.		

#5 Rejection Learnings

What did you learn from the four rejections you have listed, when they happened? Were these learnings of value?

What will you learn from the same rejections if they were to happen today? Are you better prepared to learn from rejection today, compared to earlier? What has made this change happen? Don't say 'reading this book'. What else has happened to you internally?

Rejections	Learnings Then	Learnings Now
1.		
2.		
3.		
4.		

#6 Become Rejection Positive

When the rejection happened, did you see any positive in the rejection? Or was it just a big disappointment?

If the same rejection were to happen today, what could be the positives you may be able to glean from these rejections?

Rejections	Positives Then	Positives Now
1. ……		
2. ……		
3. ……		
4. ……		

#7 Rejection Processing System

Do you now have your own rejection processing system? What are the five or six or seven steps you will follow to handle future rejections?

1. ......

2. ......

3. ......

4. ......

5. ......

6. ......

7. ......

Further Reading/Watching/Listening

Books

- *Seven Habits of Highly Effective People*—Steven Covey
- *Mindset*—Carol Dwek (also visit www.mindsetonline.com)
- *Learned Optimism*—Martin Seligman
- *Man's Search For Meaning*—Viktor E. Frankl
- *Positively Resilient*—Doug Hench
- *The Winning Attitude*—Jeff Keller
- *The Habit of Winning*—Prakash Iyer
- *Coaching For Resilience*—Adreinne Green
- *The Winning Way*—Harsha & Anita Bhogle
- *Bhagawad-gita As It Is*—A. C. Bhaktivedanta Swami Prabhupada

Articles/Blog Posts

- How Resilience Works—Diane L Coutu (HBR)
- Dealing With Rejection in Academia—Staci Zavattaro (LSE Blog)
- Do you keep a failure résumé?—Tim Herrera (NYT Blog)
- Rejection—A Loser's Guide—Adoree Drayappah (Blog)
- How to bounce back from Adversity—Joshua Margois (HBR.org)
- Rebounding from career setback—Mitchell Lee Marks (HBR)

Audio/Video

- Emotional First Aid—Guy Winch (TEDx Video) (Book: *Emotional First Aid*—Guy Winch)
- How to Bounce Back from Rejection—Adam Grant (Podcast)
- What I learnt from 100 days of rejection—Jia Jiang (TEDx Video) (Book: *Rejection Proof*—Jia Jiang)

Movies

Numerous movies and television mini-series follow what Joseph Campbell described in his book *Hero With A Thousand Faces* as the hero's journey; where a hero who starts out as someone one who is in a good place, faces imminent death or rejection or failure, but rises above all odds to become successful. Sometimes he is helped by the people around him, or by a divine power (in mythologies). Often it his own inner calling that helps him win the battle. Here is a list of just a few movies. There are many more.

- *Jerry McGuire*
- *Star Wars*
- *It's a Wonderful Life*
- *Joy (Miracle Mop Story)*
- *Chak De India* (Hindi)

Acknowledgements

When the first two copies of my book (*FCB Ulka Brand Building Advertising—Concepts & Cases*) arrived at my desk in March 2001, I was thrilled to bits. But little did I know that in a span of less than two decades I would end up writing ten books covering topics ranging from branding and consumer behaviour to advertising and leadership lessons.

However, this book of mine is different and its core target reader is a little different from those of my previous nine books.

As you may have read in the first chapter of the book, this book was triggered by a question I was asked at a university in Bhopal. That question led to a whole new stream of ideas and conversations. And so this book is not just about the world of marketing and advertising. It is about facing rejection and failure, and bouncing back with renewed energy.

Like a spring.

So the first thanks should go to my wife, Nithya and my literary agent, Anish Chandy for pushing me out of my comfort zone of writing about brands, advertising and clients.

As I started my quest for stories around rejection, I went back to my own experiences in campuses and companies. I was also able to spend time with several leaders who generously offered their time to discuss the topic of rejection. I would like to express my deepest gratitude specifically to Mr M. Damodaran, former Chairman, SEBI and CMD IDBI, Prof. Ranjan Banerjee, Dean of SPJIMR, Viren Rasquinha, Olympian and CEO of Olympic Gold Quest, R. Sridhar, CEO, Coach and Former Director, Ogilvy & Mather. All of them were generous with their time and suggestions and this book would not be what it is without their inputs.

My search for stories around rejection led me to browse through not less than twenty books and around fifty articles of varying lengths. Some of those books and articles have been highlighted in the book and I am grateful to all these wise authors for showing me the light. Given the fact that I am no psychologist or psychiatrist, the books and articles were of invaluable help, even to decode my own rejection experiences.

The book, like my previous two books started as a discussion with my literary agent, Anish Chandy of Labyrinth Literary Agency. Special thanks to Gautam Padmanabhan of Westland for his unstinting support. I enjoyed working with Radhakrishan Nair, Arunima Mazumdar, Shweta Bhagat, Team Moes-Art during the launch of my book *Sponge: Leadership Lessons I Learnt From My Clients* (also published by Westland). I look forward to working with them again.

In Karthik Venkatesh I had a wonderful editor who managed to spot things that I end up overlooking, correct the numerous mistakes I had made and also point out inaccuracies and inadequacies.

The stunning cover design is by Gavin Morris; special thanks to him for a very striking cover.

The book is really the result of many conversations I have had with many friends. In particular, Isaac Jacob, Arun Kale,

Kinjal Medh, R. Sridhar, Gauri Chaudhary, my son Aditya, Himanshu Parmekar, Amit Doshi (IVM Podcast) and others. All of them offered to read and comment on the early drafts of the book. Special thanks to them for their valuable inputs.

Finally, this book started with a question from a twenty-year-old student in Bhopal. I do hope the book will be of help to her and to the young and old as they navigate the new world around us. If you find the stories of interest and value, credit should go to the many experts I spoke with and books and articles I managed to read. The faults are entirely mine.

Veteran adman and author Ambi Parameswaran has relied on one process of learning above all others: powerful conversations with clients and customers. A challenging customer, in his view, goes from being someone who poses an obstacle to quality work to someone with eye-opening ideas and concepts. Approached as an exercise in listening and learning, these conversations can become long-term lessons.

Ambi has worked with some of the most respected brands and names in the Indian corporate world, and each of those assignments were for him masterclasses in leadership development. In this book, Ambi recounts conversations with some of the most iconic business leaders, such as Ratan Tata, Azim Premji, S. Ramadorai, Karsanbhai Patel, M. Damodaran, Dr V. Kurien and many others. He soaked up these conversations, in his own words, 'like a sponge'.

This book is an attempt to walk us through some of those dialogues – both the illuminating and the difficult aspects of them – to help us understand how they were learning sessions. For anyone looking at turbocharging their business and career, the 'Sponge Process' that emphasises listening is a radical new way of engaging with clients and customers.

www.ingramcontent.com/pod-product-compliance
Lightning Source LLC
Chambersburg PA
CBHW070509160726
48003CB00004B/1494